Winners of the Heisman Trophy

Winners of the Heisman Trophy

John Devaney

Walker and Company
New York

For Luke R. Devaney

First published in the United States of America
in 1986 by the Walker Publishing Company, Inc.

Published simultaneously in Canada by John Wiley & Sons
Canada, Limited, Rexdale, Ontario.

*Heisman Memorial Trophy ® and likeness of the actual trophy are
registered service marks owned by the Downtown Athletic Club
under Registration Numbers 936,853 and 936,852, respectively.
"Heisman" and "Heisman Trophy Award" also are service marks
owned by the Downtown Athletic Club of New York City, Inc.

Library of Congress Cataloging-in-Publication Data

Devaney, John.
  Winners of the Heisman Trophy.

  Includes index.
  Summary: Describes the history of the Heisman trophy, the most
important trophy awarded to an amateur football player, and
includes brief biographies of the winners.
  1. Football players—United States—Biography—
Juvenile literature. 2. College sports—United States—
Juvenile literature. 3. Heisman Trophy—Juvenile
literature. [1. Football players. 2. Heisman Trophy.
3. College sports] I. Title.
GV939.A1D425 1986   796.332′092′2 [B] [920] 85-26466
ISBN 0-8027-6610-2
ISBN 0-8027-6631-5 (Reinforced)

Book Design by Teresa M. Carboni

Printed in the United States of America

10 9 8 7 6 5 4 3 2

Contents

Acknowledgment

I thank the officers of the Downtown Athletic Club and, in particular, membership secretary Marge Koenig, for their help in gathering material and photographs for this book.

J.D.
East Hampton, N.Y.

Introduction

"AND THE WINNER IS . . ."

The Heisman Trophy. It is *the* trophy of American amateur sports. Every all-American football player dreams that one day he will win the Heisman (it rhymes with iceman). Overnight, the man who wins the Heisman becomes the nation's most famous college football player. And soon after he becomes a millionaire.

Why is this trophy so important? How do you win it? Why do you become so rich after you win it? And who was Heisman?

Imagine that we are living in 1935. This was one of the misery years of the Great Depression. Factories shut their gates because few people had enough cash to buy the things that factories made. Millions of men and women had no jobs. Children stood in ragged clothes on street corners and begged for food.

"Maybe what this country needs right now," said John W. Heisman, "is something to cheer about."

John W. Heisman had been one of the first college football players, a star for Pennsylvania and Brown in the 1890s. He had been a coach for thirty-six years at Clemson and Georgia Tech. He gave to today's football the snap from center and the idea of dividing games

John W. Heisman

into four fifteen-minute periods. In 1935, he was the athletic director of the Downtown Athletic Club (DAC). The club's home was a towering skyscraper that sat on the tip of Manhattan island, facing the Statue of Liberty. The club had been organized by New York City businessmen. They cheered for baseball heroes like Babe Ruth and Dizzy Dean. Babe's homers and Dizzy's strikeouts made people forget their troubles for a few hours.

In the fall, people cheered for college football heroes—the all-Americans. But the all-Americans graduated from college and soon were forgotten. They vanished into business careers or into pro football. Pro football then was a sport few people watched.

"We need college football heroes that will be remembered," the members of the DAC told John Heisman. "Let's pick one player each year as the best player in college football. He'll be number one—and number ones are not forgotten."

John Heisman liked the idea. That fall the Downtown Athletic Club's members asked a group of sports-

The original Heisman Trophy. It resides in a showcase in the lobby of the Downtown Athletic Club.

writers to pick 1935's number one college football player. The winner was Jay Berwanger, a high-stepping running back for the University of Chicago. The club gave Jay the Downtown Athletic Club Trophy.

A year later, in September of 1936, John Heisman suddenly died. To honor the pioneer coach, the club renamed its trophy the Heisman Memorial Trophy. Ever since, as the club members had hoped, the Heisman winners—as well as their feats and skills—

Ed Smith, a football player for New York University in the 1930s, posed in 1935 for the trophy's sculptor, Frank Eliscu. Only in 1982 did Ed learn what he had posed for. The Downtown Athletic Club gave him his own copy of the trophy in appreciation.

have been remembered long after that year's all-Americans were forgotten.

In the 1940s and 1950s many National Football League teams played in front of empty seats. Pro teams knew that all-Americans would draw people to the pro games. The fans argued about how the all-Americans would perform against the pros. Fans argued the loudest about how a Heisman winner would run or pass against hardened NFL teams.

"He'll be a flop as a pro," fans said about the Heisman winner. Then the fans paid to see if they were right or wrong.

Fordham coach Jim Crowley studies a clay model of the trophy in 1935 while one of his players carries the ball as a player of the time would. Crowley suggested to the sculptor that the statue's straight arm be moved slightly, and this was done before the plaster mold was cast in bronze. From that mold have come the trophies for all the winners since Jay Berwanger in 1935.

Pro teams waved thick wads of cash in front of all-Americans to tempt them to play for one team instead of another. One team might offer an all-American $10,000 a season. Another would bid $20,000 for the same player. And if an all-American got $20,000, a Heisman winner got $30,000.

Most Heisman winners proved to be worth every dollar they got—and the dollars kept growing. Heisman winners of the 1960s, 1970s, and 1980s became pro football's most awesome scorers. Among them: Roger Staubach, O.J. Simpson, Jim Plunkett, Earl Campbell, Tony Dorsett, Marcus Allen, and Herschel Walker.

In 1984, the Heisman winner was a plucky quarterback from Boston College—Doug Flutie. A new pro football league, the United States Football League (USFL), needed to lure fans to its games. The New

Jersey Generals, a USFL team, paid Doug more than one million dollars a year—the most ever paid to a football player.

Today the Heisman is so famous that the trophy has its own television show. Each year the winner is selected by hundreds of sportswriters and broadcasters. (The author has been among them.) For days after the voting, the club keeps secret the name of the winner. On a night in New York in early December, the season's two or three top all-Americans gather in front of TV cameras at the Downtown Athletic Club. Then, as the Heisman Trophy Show begins on CBS, the winner's happy face is flashed onto the screens in millions of American homes. In 1985 that happy face was the face of Auburn's running back, Bo Jackson.

You can win the Heisman if you have skill and daring. You can win if you are fast and strong. But you can also win after people have said you were "too small"—as they said to Doug Flutie. You can win after people have said you were "too slow"—as they said to Jim Plunkett.

The Heisman is won in all kinds of ways—including, if truth be told, sometimes with just a little bit of luck. This book tells of the ways—sometimes oddball but always thrilling—that eleven young men won the Heisman.

1

Doug Flutie

"THE LITTLE RASCAL"

You are losing, 45–41, to the nation's number one team of a year ago. You have the ball on the 50-yard line. There are only six seconds left to play. What do you do?

Doug Flutie knew what he was going to do. He was going to throw a long forward pass and hope that someone on his side caught the ball for a touchdown. But Doug had a special play he wanted to call.

Doug stood only to the armpits of most of his Boston College (BC) teammates as they ducked into the huddle. "The little rascal," as his teammates called him, looked at the circle of anxious faces.

How often he had won games for them with miracle passes! Could he do it one last time?

"Fifty-five flood tip!" the narrow-eyed quarterback snapped. The Eagles trotted out of the huddle toward the line of scrimmage. Huge University of Miami defenders stared at Flutie—Goliaths awaiting David.

Doug glanced to his right. He saw his three swiftest pass catchers poised to fly down the field. One was Gerard Phelan, his best friend and roommate. Doug had practiced fifty-five flood tip with his pass receivers the day before. All three were supposed to streak toward the end zone. Doug had to hold the ball until

7

Some of the fifty-odd winners of the Heisman assemble in the Downtown Athletic Club in 1984:

Front row, left to right: John Huarte, 1964, Notre Dame; Steve Owens, 1969, Oklahoma; O. J. Simpson, 1968, USC; Herschel Walker, 1982, Georgia; Mike Rozier, 1983, Nebraska; Pat Sullivan, 1971, Auburn.

Second row: Vic Janowicz, 1950, Ohio State; Frank Sinkwich, 1942, Georgia; Les Horvath, 1944, Ohio State; Doak Walker, 1948, SMU; Doug Flutie, 1984, Boston College; Jay Berwanger, 1935, Chicago; Clint Frank, 1937, Yale; Larry Kelley, 1936, Yale; Johnny Lujack, 1947, Notre Dame.

Back row: Angelo Bertelli, 1943, Notre Dame; Howard Cassady, 1955, Ohio State; Archie Griffin, 1974 and 1975, Ohio State; John Cappelletti, 1973, Penn State; John David Crow, 1957, Texas A & M; Johnny Lattner, 1953, Notre Dame; Alan Ameche, 1954, Wisconsin; Leon Hart, 1949, Notre Dame; Doc Blanchard, 1945, Army; Pete Dawkins, 1958, Army; Dick Kazmaier, 1951, Princeton; Steve Spurrier, 1966, Florida; Gary Beban, 1967, UCLA; Terry Baker, 1962, Oregon State.

they got near the goal line. Then he would arch a high pass. If the BC receiver nearest the ball couldn't catch it, he would try to tip it high into the air. Then perhaps another BC player might latch onto it.

It was a dicey play, one that had worked only once during this 1984 season for the BC Eagles. On the sideline, Eagle coach Jack Bicknell knew how much

Doug looks for an open receiver, running away from tacklers as he did for 55 flood tip.

faith he had in this last play of the game. He was going over in his mind what to tell his players after they had lost.

"I've never thought I was too small to do anything," Doug, a high school senior, was telling his older brother Bill. "But all these college coaches say I am too small to be a college passer. Maybe they're right. How do I know? I've never played against college players."

Until now—the spring of 1981—the 5′9″, 175-pound Doug had thought he could do anything in any sport. When he was growing up in Florida, he loved sports. "If it was a rainy day and we couldn't play outdoors, Doug would make up games we could play in the basement," his brother Bill recalls. "He'd crush a paper cup and make believe it was a ball. We'd play what he called

9

Paper Cup Baseball downstairs. Our hand would be the bat that we swung at the paper cup."

Doug was born in Manchester, Maryland, on October 23, 1962. His father was an engineer who worked on computers. His father changed jobs in 1967. He and his wife took their three sons—Bill, Doug, and Darren—to Melbourne, Florida. When Dick Flutie came home from work in the afternoon, he batted baseballs to the boys. Or they played a game of touch football on a nearby beach.

"My father always pushed us to win," Doug once told me. "Dad taught us that you had to do the things necessary for being a winner—like working hard."

"It was fun to watch Doug play," his mother remembers. Once, she recalls, Doug was playing shortstop in a Little League game. There was a runner on second base. The ball was hit to Doug. He scooped up the grounder and faked a throw to first. The runner bolted toward third, thinking the ball was going toward first. Doug dived at the runner and tagged him out.

"Doug was usually the best player," his mother said. "But more than that, he was always doing the unexpected."

In 1976, Dick Flutie switched jobs again. The family moved to Natick, Massachusetts. Bill and Doug tried out for the football team at Natick High. Bill became the team's passer. Younger Doug, weighing only 150 pounds, was the team's safetyman on defense.

In one game, a 200-pound fullback blew through the line. Little Doug dived at his ankles, tripping him up. Then Doug ripped the ball out of the back's hands and ran 70 yards for a touchdown. Natick won, 6 0.

In practices the coach saw little Doug arch the football 50 and 60 yards. One day the coach told Doug's brother Bill that he was no longer the team's passer.

"Now you are going to catch passes—from your brother."

Bill didn't mind. He knew Doug would aim a lot of passes at him. In one game, Natick was losing, 25–24. There were only a few minutes left in the game. Doug whistled four straight passes into Bill's hands. Natick reached the 21-yard line. The trouble was, only three seconds remained.

Natick's quarterback called time out. "Let me kick a field goal!" Doug begged his coach.

"You've never kicked a field goal!"

"I can do it!" Doug pleaded.

"Okay," the coach said, shrugging. He had no one else who could kick a long field goal.

Doug laced on a kicking shoe. His nervous mother no longer thought he was fun to watch. She bolted out of her seat and hid under the stands. From there she heard a loud roar. She peeked at the scoreboard. Natick had won, 27–25. Doug Flutie had kicked the first—and only—field goal of his life.

No college coaches knocked at Doug's door, asking him to come to their campuses. Scouts said, "He's too small for college football. A passer that small can't see over the heads and arms of rushers who are 6'4" and bigger."

Doug stared blankly at friends when he heard what the scouts said. He'd always been good in sports. He'd beaten boys in baseball, basketball, and football who towered over him. "Height?" Doug said, shaking his head. "I never even thought about height."

One college coach badly needed a quarterback who could throw long passes. Jack Bicknell, the Boston College coach, gave Doug a four-year scholarship. Maybe this little kid could throw over bigger men. But a BC coach told Doug, "You're so small, you might not make it at quarterback. Since you're quick, we may put you on defense as a safety."

Doug just wanted to play—anywhere. In the fall of 1981, he stepped onto the green, rolling BC campus at Chestnut Hill. Early in that 1981 season, the weak Eagles lost two of their first three games. The little freshman watched from the bench.

In the fourth game, Penn State was trampling the Eagles, 38–0. Coach Bicknell said to an assistant, "Let's see what the kid can do."

Doug ran into the game. He was so scared he couldn't remember the BC plays. In the huddle he stuttered, "I-I-I'm going to pass."

On each play he ran back and just threw. One of those passes streaked into the arms of a BC end for a touchdown. BC lost, 38–7, but in the dressing room Bicknell stared at Doug and asked himself. "Is that my number one quarterback?"

Doug had won the job for the rest of the season. Each afternoon he came to practices carrying a large boxy radio/tape recorder that blared rock. "That box," a teammate told a reporter, "is almost as big as Flutie."

In the locker room he dressed quietly, rarely speaking to the players, most older than he. He grinned, blushing, when they teased him about his size. He laughed, glad to be accepted, when big linemen hoisted him off the bench with one hand and shouted, "Who wants this little kid?"

On the field, though, he was *the* boss. In huddles he snapped out commands. "For a little guy," he once said, "I've got a big mouth."

The Eagles realized he was smart. He changed plays at the line of scrimmage when he saw that the play he had called in the huddle wouldn't work against a shifting defense. Once he called for a run up the middle. At the line he saw two linebackers edge toward the middle. Doug shouted out a new play—a run to the outside. The runner swept around the end for a touchdown.

And he was nimble. He danced and darted away from tacklers who were bigger but not as quick. Then he threw touchdown passes. By the end of the 1981 season, BC's little freshman ranked number nine among all the nation's passers.

In 1981, BC had not been ranked among the country's top fifty teams. By 1983, the Eagles flew among the top ten. Newspapers hailed Doug as BC's "Little Big Man."

His last-minute touchdowns to win games thrilled BC fans. Alabama led, 31–14. Flutie rifled passes into the hands of scurrying receivers. BC won, 38–31. Rutgers led, 13–6, with a minute to play. The Eagles stood 90 yards away from a touchdown. Doug lofted passes and—*bang, bang, bang*—the Eagles leapfrogged toward the goal line. Near the goal line, Doug was trapped by tacklers as he ran back to pass. He tossed the ball under the arms of the tacklers for the touchdown. Then he lined another pass for the two-point conversion. BC won, 14–13.

In the 1983 season, his junior year, he finished third in the Heisman voting behind winner Mike Rozier of Nebraska and Brigham Young's Steve Young. "I remember as a kid watching on TV when O.J. Simpson won the Heisman," he told Gerard Phelan. "Next season I have a chance to win it. I ask myself, 'Am I dreaming or is this all really happening to me?'"

Among his friends in Natick, Doug—the football hero—was still the same bustling, laughing kid. Home from college for vacations, he scampered down to a nearby playground, gym, or vacant lot for pickup games of basketball, baseball, or softball. In the evenings he drove to a movie with his girlfriend since high school, Laurie Fortier.

Teammates often had parties on campus. Doug left early when the music and the noise got loud. "I am not much of a party man," he explained. "I like to relax."

A friend said, "Doug's idea of a big party is a hamburger and soda at Wendy's with Laura."

As the 1984 season began, most experts picked 1983's number one team, the University of Miami, to repeat as number one. Miami's rangy passer, Bernie Kosar, was thought likely to win the Heisman. Fans looked forward to the duel between Miami and BC, Kosar and Flutie, late in the season. "We'll show 'em," BC fans said, "who is number one."

Under a gloomy, drippy sky in Miami's Orange Bowl, the two quarterbacks rained passes that were grabbed for touchdowns. With six seconds left, Miami led, 45–41. In the huddle Doug called what would be the last play of the game—fifty-five flood tip. He watched Gerard Phelan and his other two fast receivers line up to the right of him.

Seconds later he faded back as Miami rushers cracked into his blockers, screaming, arms flailing. Doug stood calmly, gripping the ball. He waited for his three Eagles to get close to the goal line. A pass to the 1-yard line would not be good enough; the game's last seconds were ticking away.

A Miami tackler flew over a blocker and rocketed toward Doug. Doug stepped aside. His blockers couldn't hold the wave of rushers any longer.

Doug ran back from the 50 to the 45, then the 40, waiting, waiting for those receivers to get to the goal line. . . . Three Miami rushers bore down on him like a tidal wave. . . .

Doug whirled away, then stopped at the 38. He planted his front foot, cocked his right arm, and let the ball fly.

It flew on a humpbacked line toward the distant goalposts some 60 yards away. Passing the 10-yard line Gerard Phelan turned and saw the walnut-brown ball plunge downward from the leaden sky. Phelan leapt, both hands outstretched. The ball smacked into his hands. He crashed to the ground. When he hit that ground, the game was over. Gerard Phelan looked down to see where he had landed.

In the end zone! An official's hands were thrusting high into the air, signaling a touchdown. BC had won another miracle finish, 47–41.

Several days later Doug Flutie and Bernie Kosar sat near each other before TV cameras in New York. They had finished among the top four in the voting for the 1984 Heisman. Now they would find out which was number one and which was number two.

A Downtown Athletic Club official told millions watching on their TV screens, "The winner of the Heisman Memorial Trophy, from Boston College . . ."

Doug's father watched his son jump up, delight lighting his face that was so grim only moments earlier. "The little kid," Dick Flutie kept saying of the boy who loved to play. "The little kid . . ."

The little kid was now rich. He signed to play for the New Jersey Generals for seven million dollars over five years. He and Laurie were married.

He would always think of himself as a kid who loved to play just for the joy of it. He told me that one day as we sat in the Generals' locker room. "I can't think of myself as a star," he said. "To me, I am a guy who likes to hang around playgrounds or gyms and play whatever game everyone else is playing. My favorite hobbies are not reading books or watching TV. My hobbies are

Doug and his proud parents stand with the original Heisman, made before all of them were born.

softball and basketball. I still like to do the exact same things I did when I was twelve years old. To me, Tony Dorsett and Herschel Walker, they are stars. I would read about them in the papers, I would pay to watch them play. I'm still just an ordinary neighborhood guy who is crazy about sports."

But for the rest of his life, Doug Flutie could never be just an ordinary guy. He had won the Heisman. Forever he would be remembered as a number one.

2

Glenn Davis and Doc Blanchard

MR. INSIDE AND MR. OUTSIDE

*It's all over, Arm-eee . . . it's all over, Arm-eee . . .
your streak is gone, Arm-eee . . .*

That chant filled the packed Michigan stadium on a
fall day in 1946. Army's twenty-game winning streak,
begun in 1943 and stretched through 1944 and 1945,
at last seemed snapped.

The University of Michigan's Wolverines had just
smashed through the Army line for a touchdown, tying
the game, 13–13. The Wolverines had scored so swiftly
and savagely that they seemed likely to score again
whenever they got their hands on the ball.

Not even the fabled Mr. Inside and the awesome Mr.
Outside could save Army this day, fans told each other.

After all, the big boys are back!

Army's Mr. Inside was the 6'2", 210-pound Felix (Doc)
Blanchard, a brawny fullback and champion shot-
putter. "He's all muscle, bone, and some concrete," a
coach once joked. Mr. Inside crashed into the center of
enemy lines. Tacklers bounced off him as if he were a
tank. He carried others, clinging to his broad back,
into the end zone. "I have seen Superman," a Notre
Dame coach once said. "His name is Blanchard."

Doc Blanchard breaks loose for a 52-yard touchdown run against Navy in 1946 during his last game for Army.

Army's Mr. Outside was stick-slim 5'10", 170-pound Glenn (Junior) Davis. He ran so fast that he beat champion sprinters in track meets at Madison Square Garden. Mr. Outside took the football and shot toward the sideline. He ran away from tacklers, then turned downfield and streaked into the end zone for touchdowns—more TDs than anyone before him.

Army's foes spread out sideline to sideline to hem in Mr. Outside. Then Mr. Inside bulled through the strung-out defense. Wrote New York Sun reporter George Trevor:

> Ashes to ashes, dust to dust,
> If Mr. Inside doesn't get you,
> Mr. Outside must.

But the big boys were back!
From 1942 to 1945, Army's football team had been manned by strong, fast players like Davis and Blanchard. They were cadets training at West Point to be

Glenn Davis shows his flashing form during practice.

second lieutenants. From West Point they marched off
to fight in the battles of World War II then roaring
across Europe and the Pacific.

Army played against college teams whose best players
were already fighting in World War II. Those weakened

teams were routed by Army by scores of 83–0 and 69–7. Once-mighty Notre Dame was buried, 48–0. But this was 1946; the war was over. Schools like Notre Dame and Michigan welcomed back from the war their best players, hardened by years of fighting.

They were the big boys. They had come back to avenge those defeats by Army when the Cadets ruled in 1944 and 1945 as the nation's number one team.

Michigan's Wolverines were among the first of the big boys to get a crack at Army as the 1946 season began. As Mr. Inside and Mr. Outside waited for the kickoff in this 13–13 game, they knew they had to score quickly or walk off, humbled victims of the big boys.

Felix Blanchard was born near Bishopville, South Carolina, on April 1, 1924. His father was the town doctor. Everyone called him Doc. When people saw Felix Blanchard gallop down dusty streets playing cowboys and Indians with his pals, they smiled and said, "There goes little Doc."

In high school nobody called Felix "little" anything. At a muscled 6-foot and 190 pounds, he was just plain Doc.

By 1941 Doc Blanchard was storming through lines as a freshman fullback at the University of South Carolina. "Give the ball to Doc and he seems to explode," his coach said. "I have never seen any big man so fast off the mark."

Japanese bombs fell on Pearl Harbor in December of that year. Doc joined the Army as a private. His dad wanted him to lead troops into battle as an officer. Doc took the test for the U.S. Military Academy at West Point and passed. In the fall of 1944, Cadet Blanchard tried out for the Army football team. He heard excited talk about a flash from California named Glenn Davis.

Glenn was born the day after Christmas, December 26, 1924, in Laverne, California. He and his brother

Ralph were twins. Ralph was born minutes earlier and, for years, Glenn, the younger, was called Junior. At Bonita High School he was the basketball team's high scorer, the baseball team's speediest outfielder and best hitter, the track team's fastest sprinter. In football he ran, passed, and caught passes for touchdowns.

In the spring of 1943, he took the test for West Point and passed. All cadets had to take the Master of the Sword Test. There were ten events. They included the 300-yard run, the standing broad jump, the rope climb, bar vaulting, chinning, sit-ups, and a softball throw. The best possible score was 1,000. The average Cadet scored 540 in 1943. The best score ever until then was 901½. Glenn scored 962½—still a record at the Point four decades later.

One afternoon in 1943, the Dodgers, then in Brooklyn, played a practice baseball game against the Cadets. Glenn bunted for a single and then stole second, third, and home. From centerfield he rifled throws that cut down five Dodger runners. After the game the stunned Dodger boss, Branch Rickey, walked up to Glenn and said, "I'll sign you for the Dodgers tomorrow."

Glenn stayed a cadet. In the 1943 season, he scored an average of one touchdown a game. And that season Army began its streak of unbeaten games.

Doc joined Glenn in the backfield at the start of the 1944 season. Until then the most famous number ever worn by a football player had been Red Grange's 77, when the Galloping Ghost ran wild for Illinois in the 1920s. Only one of the previous Heisman winners had a famous numeral. He was Michigan's rampaging tailback, Tom Harmon, who won in 1940. His 88 was almost as famous as Grange's 77.

Chicago's fleet runner, Jay Berwanger, had won the first Heisman in 1935, but his 99 was soon forgotten. So were the numbers of Yale's pass catcher, Larry

Kelley, the 1936 winner; his passer, Clint Frank (1937); TCU's little quarterback, Davey O'Brien (1938); and Iowa's runner, passer, and drop-kicker, Nile Kinnick, who won in 1939 and died only four years later when his fighter plane crashed in the Pacific during World War II.

Then came Harmon and the 1940s. Minnesota's fullback, Bruce Smith, won in 1941; Georgia's passer and runner, Frank Sinkwich, in 1942; and Notre Dame's rifle passer, Angelo Bertelli, in 1943. None had well-known numerals. But by the end of 1944, nearly every schoolboy in knickers or in his first long pants knew that Number 41 was Glenn Davis, Mr. Outside, and Number 35 was Doc Blanchard, Mr. Inside.

In their first game, against North Carolina, Mr. Outside flashed 73, 38, and 37 yards for three touchdowns. Mr. Inside's only touchdown was the most spectacular. Glenn threw a pass to end Barney Poole, who was trapped. Barney lateralled the ball to Doc and Doc sprinted 60 yards for the touchdown. Army won, 46–0.

That was a typical Army victory as the Cadets swept unbeaten through the 1944 season. Glenn scored almost three touchdowns a game, for a total of twenty that led the nation. He averaged almost 12 yards a carry, a college record forty years later. He and Doc were on almost everyone's all-American team. Glenn finished second in the voting for the Heisman behind Ohio State's veteran halfback, Les Horvath. Doc was third.

"I never thought I had a chance of winning," said Les, who had gained 5.7 yards a rush. He had beaten Glenn by only 125 votes. What helped Les was his passing for six touchdowns. Glenn had become the first sophomore to come so close to winning the Heisman.

Number 41 is Mr. Outside, number 35 is Mr. Inside.

Off the field and between seasons, Glenn and Doc were good friends but not close pals. Doc loved Army life. He marched erectly, arms swinging, shoulders braced. He wore the stripes on his sleeve of a Cadet officer. When President Roosevelt died in April of 1945, Cadet Felix Blanchard marched in the Honor Guard that carried the late President to his grave. Doc was a soldier's soldier.

Glenn, a rebel at heart, hated being enclosed in the confines of Army discipline. He muttered when he had to march on the parade ground. He had to force himself to shout, "Sir," to upperclassmen only a year older than he was. When ordered to do twenty push-ups as a punishment, he did them swiftly—but glowered as he did them.

To a friend he said, "I am a worrier. I worry about my grades. I get up early to study but I have trouble with math. I worry about football and the next game. Doc takes everything in stride. Nothing much bothers him."

Only nightmares bothered Doc. Before a game he tossed in his sleep. He would wake up a roommate as he shouted, "Tackle him! There he goes! Tackle him!"

Glenn's twin, Ralph, was also a cadet at West Point. Doc and Ralph were shot-putters on the track team. "Doc and Ralph are like a couple of puppies," the track coach once said. "Always foolin' and rasslin' around."

In 1945, the Cadets marched over opponents, conquering everyone, to stretch their unbeaten string to eighteen. Doc scored nineteen touchdowns, Glenn ran and passed for eighteen. Both played on defense, tackling runners and intercepting passes. After Army crushed Navy, 32–13, the Cadets' Long Gray Line stood and cheered when word came from New York: Felix

Doc Blanchard accepts his Heisman after the 1945 season. He said he would have voted for Glenn Davis.

(Doc) Blanchard had become the first West Pointer to win the Heisman Trophy. A close second for the second straight year: Glenn Davis.

Doc was the first junior to win the trophy. As he accepted it, he said in his soft drawl, "I would have voted for Glenn Davis."

The 1946 season would be the last for the two seniors. Mr. Inside and Mr. Outside knew that the big boys were back from the war, older and brawnier than when they had gone away as college kids. The big boys were really grown men. And those men had scores to settle with Army and Mr. Inside and Mr. Outside— embarrassing scores like 48–0 and 69–7. Each time

Army went onto the field in 1946, the big boys stood grimly, eager to swat the Cadets onto the seats of their shiny black and gold pants.

The Michigan fans roared as the Wolverines kicked off to Army, the game tied 13–13. "Stop the Arm-*eee*!" they chanted. "Stop the Arm-*eee*!" If Michigan could hold that line, then get back the ball, Army's twenty-game winning streak seemed over.

Mr. Inside and Mr. Outside knew what they had to do: keep the ball, move it downfield, and score, using up time. Then when Michigan got the ball, there'd be no time to score.

Doc slammed into the line for 3, 4, and 5 yards. Glenn dashed outside, sprinting 10, 15, and 20 yards before he was shoved out of bounds. Army slammed some 70 yards to the Michigan 7.

"Hold that line! Hold that line!" Michigan rooters screamed. When Army had the ball only 7 yards from the goal line, most everyone knew what would happen next—a charge up the middle by Mr. Inside.

Sure enough, the quarterback gave the ball to Doc. He vanished into a mob of dark-shirted Wolverines. He came out of the mob with two tacklers hanging onto his waist and another two clinging to his knees. Doc carried all four into the end zone for the winning touchdown. Army rode home still unbeaten.

One giant stood in the way of a third-straight unbeaten season: once-again-mighty Notre Dame, loaded with some fifty players who would one day be pros. Some 60,000 fans filled Yankee Stadium in New York to witness what was called "The Game of the Half-Century."

The two longtime foes struggled around midfield for much of the first half. Each line stood as hard as concrete. But then Doc broke through a crack and

Doc Blanchard became one of Texas's best amateur golfers.

Glenn quit the Army after four years. In the early 1950s he ran and caught passes for the Los Angeles Rams. He dated Hollywood's most beautiful actresses, among them a dark-haired teenager, Elizabeth Taylor.

In 1953, his knee aching, Glenn left the Rams to join a Los Angeles newspaper as director of special events, a job he held for more than thirty years. He married a beauty queen from Louisiana. He and Ellen were often seen at the big sports events in Los Angeles, including the 1984 Olympics. At that Olympic Games, a sportscaster spotted him in the stands and called him "the greatest football player of his era."

Some fans would argue that Doc Blanchard was at least as great as Glenn. They could be right. But this is a given: No college football team has ever had two runners who could do more to win a game than the Army team of Mr. Inside and Mr. Outside.

3

Doak Walker

"THE GREATEST FOOTBALL PLAYER EVER"

The Texas Christian University (TCU) ball carrier plunged into the end zone. *Touchdown!* TCU fans filled the Cotton Bowl in Dallas with the joy of their whoops.

It seemed unbelievable. TCU now led Southern Methodist University (SMU), 19–13. There was less than a minute to play. A few hours before this amazing upset, people had said, "There is no way—*no way*—that TCU can beat SMU." Cold, hard facts told them that.

Look at the record. TCU had lost more games than it had won during the 1947 season. Then look at SMU's record—unbeaten. And it had that all-American, Doak Walker. The Doaker, as SMU fans called him, threw for touchdowns. He caught passes for touchdowns. He ran—O how he ran—for touchdowns. And if he couldn't score by running and passing and catching, he won by kicking—field goals, extra points, punts—it made no difference to the Doaker. And he found ways to win by tackling runners and intercepting passes. He played thirty minutes of almost every game on offense, and thirty minutes of almost every game on defense.

But now the Doaker was silent as he walked back up the field to await TCU's kickoff. Sixty seconds to go and he was behind by a touchdown.

An exultant TCU lineman saw the somber look on the Doaker's face. He ran up to him and shouted, "Well, Doak, what are you going to do now?"

He shouldn't have said that, and maybe he wished the rest of his life that he hadn't. The Doaker stared him in the eyes and said, "We're going to score again."

His father would have grinned if he'd heard that. When Doak was born in Dallas on January 1, 1927, his father was asked if he wanted his boy to grow up to be president. "No," said Ewell Walker, a school teacher. "He's going to be an all-American football player."

When Doak was six, his dad taught him to play chess. But his father never let him forget his own favorite game, which he had played in high school. Ewell still growled to himself about how much better a football player he wished he had been. Once, playing chess, Ewell said to Doak, "Football is a chess game. You must get your opponent out of position. When you have two strong men who are physically even, the man who makes the fewest mistakes will win."

Doak never forgot that—in football or in chess. To his dad's delight, he began to win their chess matches.

Doak was a skinny, long-legged 5'9" tall, 140-pound runner at Highland Park High in Dallas. Tacklers towered over him as they tried to run him down. Doak faked left and went right. Tacklers grasped air as he flitted by. When they hit Doak, they hit at awkward angles. They couldn't get a full hold and he often wiggled away.

"A quick small man," he told a teammate, "should always be able to fool a slower big man so he gets only a piece of you."

Don't make mistakes and you win.

The Highland Park quarterback was a blond, broad-shouldered laughing boy. His name was Bobby Layne. Doak and he were pals. In games Bobby threw long passes. The rangy Doak ran under them for touchdowns. Bobby gave the ball to Doak who zigzagged for more touchdowns. When Bobby graduated, Doak became the team's passer. He was also its kicker and, on defense, its safety, roaming the field to pluck down enemy passes.

Bobby went to the University of Texas in Austin. Doak picked SMU, a Dallas school. He wanted his dad to be able to see all his games. In 1945, Doak's freshman year, SMU played Texas. Doak's running and passing and kicking put SMU ahead, 7–6. Late in the game Bobby Layne arched a long pass. Doak raced downfield with the Texas pass catcher. The ball soared over Doak's head. The Texas receiver snared it for the winning touchdown.

Bobby grinned at his old buddy after the game. Doak smiled. He promised he would get even.

But he had to wait. He went into the Army in 1946. In 1947, he came back to SMU, now 5'10" and 170 pounds, with long legs and arms like whips. After Doak's first game as a sophomore, against Missouri in the Cotton Bowl, Dallas people swore there had never been anything like him.

He leaped across the line from the 2 for a touchdown. He tossed a pass for another touchdown. He zigged and zagged 74 yards for a third. A fourth run in that game installed him in a lot of memories. He took the long snap from the center at his tailback position in SMU's single-wing formation. He swept to the right behind a wall of blockers. Missouri linemen cut down his blockers. Doak was trapped at the sideline by three Tigers.

He flashed to his left, spinning away from clutching hands and swinging fists. He outran tacklers to the left sideline and sprinted to the 50. There, panting and wide-eyed, he was trapped again. Giants pounded at him from behind. Others massed in front of him. A tackler veered toward him from the side.

Doak faked going forward. The veering tackler shot by him—an arrow off its mark. Doak flew through the open space toward the right sideline, angling toward the goal line. Tacklers chased after him, foxes after the hare that had to be tiring and slowing down.

The foxes caught up at the 20 and knocked him out of bounds. Forty years later that z-shaped run was still called the greatest in Cotton Bowl history.

"You've got to see the Doaker," people told each other in Dallas. During the next three years, so many wanted to see him that the Cotton Bowl had to be enlarged with 30,000 new seats. They came to see the Doaker—and rarely did he disappoint.

SMU leads Oklahoma State, 21–14. A State runner scoots up the middle, a blocker in front of him. Only the Doaker can stop the tying touchdown. The blocker lunges at Doak, a flying desk crashing at a straw. But the straw leans—the desk flies by. Doak wrestles down the runner. SMU wins. The play is called the best defensive play of the 1947 season. *The man who makes the fewest mistakes. . .*

SMU against UCLA. Doak runs for a touchdown. He kicks the extra point. The score stays 7–0 until late in the game. UCLA is driving for the tying touchdown. UCLA fumbles. Defensive back Doak Walker pounces on the tumbling ball. SMU 7, UCLA zip. *The man who makes the fewest mistakes. . .*

Then comes Texas, Bobby Layne, and a bad memory. Bobby throws for a TD. Doak throws for a TD and kicks the extra point. Score: Texas 7, SMU 7. The Doaker arches a long pass to a receiver who weaves his way to the Texas 38.

The Doaker huddles with coach Matty Bell. They decide on a surprise. Into the game comes Gil Johnson, whose specialty is throwing passes.

The Old Man, as teammates call the balding Gil, takes Doak's place at tailback. Doak lines up as an end.

The Doaker as a kicker. He also intercepted passes and tackled runners.

Bobby Layne and the other Texas defenders stare at each other. *What's going on?*

The ball is snapped back from the center to the Old Man. Doak charges at the Texas defenders. They don't know what he is going to do—this passer suddenly turned pass catcher.

Doak angles toward the sideline. The Old Man aims a pass that floats in the air. Doak and a Texas back leap high for the ball. Doak snatches it from the hands of the back. He comes down running, and sprints to the 1-yard line before he is knocked down. On the next play an SMU back crashes over for the touchdown. Doak kicks the extra point. SMU wins, 14–13. The Doaker and Bobby Layne are even.

Later in that 1947 season, SMU faced defeat for the first time. Underdog TCU led 19–13. There was only a minute to play. And as Doak stood waiting for the kickoff, the promise that he had made to a TCU lineman—*"We're going to score again!"*—rang in his mind.

TCU kicked off. Doak caught the ball near his goal line. His long legs flew over the grass. He leaped over tacklers. Near the 40 he charged by the SMU bench. Hemmed in by tacklers, he spun away for a moment to shout at Coach Bell: "Send in the old man!" Moments later he was buried under more than 500 pounds of TCU manpower.

Doak's 56-yard kickoff return put the ball in TCU territory. Gil Johnson ran into the game. Doak told him to throw a pass.

Now it was TCU's turn to be befuddled. What was Doak doing out there as an end? And what would he do?

He ran deep, flashing by a defender. Gil threw a long pass. Doak reached out and palmed the ball as he tumbled to the ground at the 9.

Only seconds were left as SMU huddled. Another pass, Doak ordered. He ran out. A pack of TCU backs surrounded him. They never saw the SMU receiver cut to the other side. Johnson lobbed the ball to the open receiver for the touchdown that tied the game 19–19. True to the Doaker's promise, SMU had scored again—in less than sixty seconds.

A panting Doak missed the extra point. Limp SMU fans left the Cotton Bowl happily. "Neither team," wrote Blackie Sherrod, a Dallas writer, "deserved to lose." And SMU was still unbeaten.

Nobody beat SMU's Mustangs that year. Doak finished third in the Heisman voting behind the winner, Notre Dame's Johnny Lujack, and Michigan's Bob Chappius. "He's only a soph," people in Dallas said. "The Doaker will win it next year."

The next year, 1948, SMU won ten of eleven games. Doak did everything again—passing, kicking, running, tackling, intercepting. Once a traffic jam delayed him. He came to a game a few minutes before it started. "It's okay," said a pressbox comic. "The Doaker just came down from the stands where he was selling programs."

"Doak specializes in only one thing," someone else said. "That's making miracles."

At season's end the word came from New York. Doak Walker had become the second junior (Doc Blanchard was the first) to win the Heisman. Accepting the award, Doak told the Downtown Athletic Club officials: "My father told me a long time ago that just when you think you are pretty good, someone will come along and trip you up. So while I appreciate this award, I know you can't live on what you have done in the past but what you are going to do now—and in the future."

Back in Dallas, he was the idol of every man, woman, and child. Lean and handsome, clad in his varsity sweater and creased slacks, books tucked at his side, he walked the campus with a smile for anyone who said hi. "Doak was the classic hero," a Dallas reporter once wrote. He didn't drink or smoke. He scribbled autographs for little boys and girls who stared upward, their eyes shining. He visited schools and told teenagers, their mouths agape, to drink lots of milk and eat green vegetables. He told them he was not especially

The Doaker as a passer. He was also a memorable runner.

fast nor especially strong. "But I learned how to be shifty and go left or right on a dime. You can learn, too." *Don't make mistakes and you win.*

Dallas businessmen poured awards on him. "In Dalls," someone said, "Doak was this century's Davey Crockett." Davey was one of the heroes of the nineteenth-century battle that still made Texas eyes melt—the Alamo.

"When Doak's name is mentioned at meetings," joked one Dallas executive, "we stand at attention and salute."

In 1949, Doak was hurt and played little. He heard

The 1948 winner of the Heisman, Doak Walker.

that he might be picked for the all-American team for a
third straight year. Doak wrote to the editors of
Collier's Magazine, who chose the team back then. He
said he didn't deserve to be picked. The editors recalled

all the Doak Walker miracles of the previous two seasons. They picked Doak anyway.

At 5'10" and 170 pounds, Doak was too small for the bruising pro game, people said. The Detroit Lions selected him in the draft. Doak joined his high school buddy, Bobby Layne, who was now the Lion quarterback. In 1950, his rookie season, Doak caught Bobby's passes. He ran. He kicked extra points and field goals. He led the NFL in scoring. The Lions won the NFL championship in 1952 and 1953. In 1955, Doak again topped the league in scoring.

Then, only twenty-eight years old, he retired. "I want to get out," he explained, "while I still have all my teeth and both my knees."

He was not forgotten. In 1971, *Sport Magazine* picked Doak Walker as college football's best player of the previous quarter-century. *Sports Illustrated* placed him on its All-Century backfield with Red Grange and O. J. Simpson.

Doak went on to become a well-to-do business executive in Denver. His wife, Skeeter, was a former ski champion. Together they were often seen flying down the ski slopes near Steamboat Springs, Colorado, where they had a home. "If I had discovered skiing first," Doak told a visitor one day in 1985, "I might never have played football."

Don't you believe that for a moment. Once, sitting behind a desk in his Denver office, he glanced at a calendar. "It's October—football season," he said. "When I think of playing football, I hear the crack of pads and leather, and my palms sure get sweaty."

Come October in Dallas, when fans stare down at the green of the Cotton Bowl, other palms get sweaty. Because on that green field those fans are remembering a z-shaped run and a miracle man everyone called the Doaker.

4

Paul Hornung

THE GOLDEN BOY

There is one thing you must understand about the Golden Boy. He was a winner. Always was—at least until one awful moment. "I always wanted to be with winners in college," he once told a friend. "That's why I went to Notre Dame, because they nearly always won."

And now he was losing. Losing in front of the biggest crowd—almost 60,000 people—ever to watch Notre Dame at a home game. A gritty bunch of Iowa Hawkeyes had invaded the stadium at South Bend, Indiana, and shoved the Irish around for a good part of the game. Iowa led, 14—7, and there were fewer than eight minutes left to play.

Paul Hornung stood under the Notre Dame goal-posts, waiting for the Iowa team to kick off. Iowa had just scored and jumped ahead. Paul knew the Hawk-eyes would rush down the field to topple the ball carrier.

He also knew who would carry back the ball. Himself. All during this 1955 season, the Golden Boy, as Notre Dame fans proudly called him, had run with the ball, thrown the passes, and kicked the field goals that won games for the Irish. Only once had they lost. Notre Dame ranked among the nation's top ten teams. But if this upstart Iowa team won, Notre Dame would sink to thirtieth or maybe fortieth place.

The Golden Boy had always been at the top. In sports he was his baseball team's best pitcher, his basketball team's best shooter, his football team's best everything. In the classroom he got A's. Girls' eyes followed when the blond, curly-haired, green-eyed giant strode by.

Losing. He hated the word. Maybe he could snatch this kickoff and run it back 100 yards for a touchdown.

The ball arched downward toward his outstretched hands. He caught it and ran straight up the middle, then curved toward the sideline. He flew past the 20, the 25, the 30. He heard feet pounding behind him. A weight like a sledgehammer drove against his knees. Grass rushed up at him.

He had been flattened. He looked at the sideline marker. He'd gone only 23 yards—to his own 35. Sixty-five yards—and a grinning bunch of Hawkeyes—stood between him and the victory he wanted so badly.

He was born on December 23, 1935, in Louisville, Kentucky. His mother and father separated when he was two and he was raised by his mother, who worked as an employment director for the United States Army at a depot in Louisville.

Paul grew husky and tall. In the sixth grade at St. Patrick's Grammar School, he towered over the other twelve-year-olds at tryouts for the school's football team. No one could throw or kick the ball as far, or run with it as fast as Paul.

"You'll be our quarterback," the coach said. Paul tossed for touchdowns as the team's T-formation quarterback. He shot straight ahead for more TDs. And when St. Patrick's was stopped, he stepped back and his foot thumped field goals.

At thirteen, Paul was playing second base for an American Legion baseball team filled with eighteen-year-olds.

41

"I wasn't big enough or strong enough to hit the fastballs that eighteen-year-olds threw," he once said in his easy Kentucky drawl. "But I was quick and I had a good arm, so the team wanted me for my fielding."

The boy second baseman leaped over eighteen-year-olds to make double plays. Paul's team went all the way to the American Legion World Championship at Dayton, Ohio. There it lost—to a pitcher, Chuck Stobbs, who later became a big leaguer.

At Flaget High School in Louisville, Paul was the baseball team's fastest pitcher. "I was very fast and very wild," Paul often said. And then he told one of those crazy stories he loved to tell about himself: "I gave up so many walks, I was the only pitcher ever to lose a no-hitter by the score of thirteen to twelve."

Paul seemed always to be laughing. He joked with the girls who flocked around him. "It's going to be tough sledding today," he told a girl on the way to a class.

"You didn't do your homework?" she asked, looking at him anxiously.

"No. It's just that it'll be tough sledding today because there is no snow."

Paul didn't have to worry about his classroom work. He always got A's at Flaget High and ranked among the top ten in his class. He would read a chapter in a book, close the book, then rattle off most of the facts. "He spends a half-hour on his homework, then goes off with a girl to the movies," a friend complained. "He gets an A in a test. I spend three hours and get a C."

As Flaget's quarterback, Paul ran, passed, and kicked the team to the state championship. Dozens of colleges pleaded with him to come to their campuses. Paul knew that Notre Dame had an all-American quarterback—Ralph Guglielmi, later a pro star with the Washington Redskins. But Paul wanted to be with winners. He chose Notre Dame.

Notre Dame coach Terry Brennan made Paul a full-back. In 1954, his sophomore season, Paul broke through lines for an average of almost 7 yards a try. He also played on defense, hovering behind the line as a safety to intercept passes or tackle touchdown-bound runners. He was also the team's punter. In a game against Navy, Notre Dame stopped a Navy drive only five yards from a touchdown. Paul had to kick the Irish out of danger. Notre Dame led, 6–0. A weak kick would put Navy within striking distance of the Irish goal and a touchdown that could be the winner.

Paul stood in his end zone. He grabbed the ball spiraled to him by the center. Navy linemen rushed—a blue tidal wave. Paul stepped forward and boomed the ball. It soared on the fly almost 75 yards.

Navy had to start from its own 39. The Midshipmen drove relentlessly for that winning touchdown, pushing back the Irish. But near the goal line Paul soared high to intercept a last-gasp Navy pass and save the 6–0 victory.

When the 1955 season began, Ralph Guglielmi was with the Redskins. Paul stepped in as the Irish quarterback. Each afternoon he studied films of the defenses Notre Dame would see. Paul noticed that the most of the teams had weak tacklers in the middle of their lines.

In Notre Dame's first game he took the snap from center and bolted up the middle. He gained 20 yards. He tried another quick run through the middle and gained 15 yards. Later he said, "As the T-formation quarterback, I was the closest to their weak spot. I figured I could get a lot of yardage bursting quickly up the middle."

His charges up the middle gained an average of 5 yards a try that season. When defenders moved into the middle to stop him, Paul lobbed passes over the bunched-up defenders to his circling receivers. When

Notre Dame was stopped near a goal line, Paul rammed the ball between the uprights for a three-point field goal. Rarely did he miss from inside the 25-yard line.

On defense, he roamed behind the line as the free safety. If a runner shot by everyone else. Paul struck him down. If a pass catcher got by everyone else, Paul latched onto him. "No one on our team," Coach Brennan said, "has more pressure on his shoulders than Paul."

Since Doak Walker in 1948, most Heisman winners had been double- and triple-threats. Notre Dame end Leon Hart (1949) could carry the ball and catch it. Ohio State back Vic Janowicz (1950) ran, passed, and kicked field goals. Princeton back Dick Kazmaier (1951) ran and passed. Oklahoma back Billy Vessels (1952) ran and passed. Notre Dame back Johnny Lattner (1953) ran the ball and caught passes. Only the 1954 winner, Wisconsin fullback Alan (The Horse) Ameche, was strictly a runner.

No previous winner since Doak Walker, however, could kick with Paul's accuracy. None could run swifter or dodge more cleverly. Paul could catch passes as well as anybody—and throw them more accurately. When someone else carried the ball, his fullback's body made him one of 1955's most fearsome blockers. On defense, he tackled as hard as a lineman, batted away or intercepted passes as dependably as any safety in the country.

In the 1955 season, Notre Dame beat eight of its first nine opponents, losing only to Michigan State. But now an aroused Iowa Hawkeye bunch stood within arm's reach of taking home one of the season's most astonishing upsets. Iowa had just tripped up Paul as he returned a kickoff. Iowa led, 14—7. Paul and his teammates stood 65 yards away from a tie. Even if they scored a touchdown, they'd have to score again to win. And there were only eight minutes left to do all that . . .

Paul shows the running form that made him one of Notre Dame's greatest runners. His arm was not strong enough nor accurate enough, however, for Paul to succeed as a passer in the National Football League. He did become one of the NFL's most consistent ground gainers as a runner.

Paul guessed that the Hawkeyes would expect him to throw long passes to get a quick touchdown. In the huddle he told his team he was going to throw short passes over the middle or to the sidelines.

Paul took the snap at the Irish 35, curled backward, then lined a diagonal pass to end Gene Kapish, who battled to the Iowa 47. He tossed another angled pass to back Dick Fitzgerald, who scooted to the 32.

The Notre Dame fans stood, screaming. Iowa fans thundered for the Hawkeyes to hold. In the huddle Paul had to shout out the next play. He now figured that Iowa would loosen up its defense, falling back to knock down those passes. Paul faded back to pass. He saw the defenders retreat. Paul stuffed the ball into the hands of Dick Fitzgerald. The big fullback burst through the scattered defense. He shot to the 19.

Paul glanced at the clock. Fewer than five minutes left. He had to work fast. He decided to give Iowa what it had originally expected but had now forgotten about—the long pass.

He ran back, all the way to the 38, waiting for one of his receivers to shake himself loose. He saw end Jim Morse cut by an Iowa defender at the 10. Paul's right arm whipped through the air. Jim Morse caught the ball at the 2. He raced into the end zone, arms flung high. Paul coolly kicked the extra point. Notre Dame 14, Iowa 14. Notre Dame fans roared so loud the stadium seemed to shake.

Iowa tried to score. Paul and the Notre Dame defense held firm. Iowa had to punt. In the huddle Paul sensed that Iowa didn't know what he would try next. He told Jim Morse to try to shake loose as he had done on the touchdown play.

Paul stepped back. He saw Jim fly away from an Iowa defender. Paul lined a pass into Jim's arms, and Jim raced all the way to the Iowa 9. Penalties pushed the Irish back to the 28. It was fourth down.

Paul had to try for a field goal, victory riding on his right foot. Calmly, he eyed the distant goalposts from where the ball would be set down—almost 40 yards away. Back came the ball. It was placed on the grass. Incoming Iowa defenders ran straight at Paul, screaming, arms waving. Paul's eyes were fixed on the ball. He strode forward and kicked. The ball shot upward, tumbled end over end, then arched downward—right between the posts.

Field goal! Some two minutes later the game ended, Notre Dame 17–14 comeback winners. Jubilant Notre Dame students carried Paul off the field on their shoulders.

The next season, 1956, Notre Dame had graduated many of its best players. Others were hurt. Opponents smashed by the weak Notre Dame blocking. "Paul would go back to pass," said former ND quarterback Angelo Bertelli, "and he'd either have to hurry his throw or run with it. Most of the time he ran."

Paul Hornung sits for a portrait a few weeks after winning the Heisman in 1956. "If only good looks counted," a reporter wrote, "Paul Hornung would have won the Heisman three years in a row."

Notre Dame won only two of its ten games, but Paul gained 1,337 yards, second highest in the nation. When time came to vote for the Heisman, voters saw no one outstanding. They remembered last year when Paul had finished fifth behind Ohio State's runner Howard (Hopalong) Cassady in the voting for the Heisman. In a close vote, Paul beat out Tennessee runner Johnny Majors for the trophy. A surprised Paul said, "After that bad a season, I didn't think I was up for consideration. I was lucky, I guess, that no one else had a sensational year."

Paul had become the first player to win the Heisman after his team had a losing season. Ironically, the guy who had always yearned to be with winners had ended his college career with losers. But *he* had won the Heisman to go off a winner.

He went on winning as a halfback and field goal kicker for Coach Vince Lombardi's Green Bay Packers. Green Bay won the world championship in 1961, 1962, and 1965. Paul was suspended one year for betting on football games, a mistake he didn't make again. In 1966, he retired. His blond handsomeness and radiant

47

smile got him jobs in front of TV cameras. He helped to telecast Notre Dame and pro football games. The Golden Boy's charm made him a salesman for coal and real-estate companies in Louisville, where he lived. Each year, at Kentucky Derby time in Louisville, Paul was seen at trackside with a beautiful lady on his arm.

Paul was among the last of the Triple Threats—those players who could run, pass, and kick. In the 1960s, coaches began to look for players who could do one thing—run or pass or kick—but who could do it with super skill. As a Packer, Paul proved he was a super runner. But when he was The Golden Boy at Notre Dame, "Paul Hornung could do more things," Vince Lombardi once said, "than any man who ever played this game."

5

Roger Staubauch

"LIKE TRYING TO
TACKLE THE WIND"

The 100,000 people in the Philadelphia stadium let out an expectant roar. Navy led 15–6 in this 1962 game. It was *the* game for both teams—Army against Navy. Their commander in chief, President John F. Kennedy, watched from the stands. Anything could happen between these two rivals. Each team desperately wanted to win. The season would be a success for the team that won, a disaster for the team that lost.

Navy's lanky quarterback, Roger Staubach, leaned over his center and scanned the Army defense. It was third down. He knew the Army was looking for a pass. He saw two hulking linebackers edge forward, ready to charge at him from the left side.

OK, that's OK.

He took the snap and ran back into his pocket of blockers. The linebackers flashed through the pocket from the left. Roger ducked to his right. The linebackers shot by him, their hands clutching air.

Roger looked at the left sideline. He saw two of his pass catchers streak down the sideline. Army's pass defenders swung toward the left side.

Just what he wanted them to do!

The two linebackers skidded to a stop, wheeled, and charged back at Roger from his blind side. He heard

Roger calls the signals for Navy.

their pounding feet. He ducked. The linebackers soared over his helmet like rockets.

Roger stood. In his mind the play was flashing like quick scenes in a movie. The defense was flowing to the left—*so there had to be a Navy pass catcher alone on the right.*

But where was he?

An Army tackler broke by a blocker. He grabbed Roger's arm. Roger tried to spin away but now he was going down.

Roger had always liked to fool tacklers and run with the ball. As a boy in Cincinnati, where he was born on February 5, 1942, he was the fastest in his neighborhood. In baseball games he liked to steal bases. Sometimes when he was trapped between bases he'd jump back and forth until someone threw the ball away. Rarely was he tagged out.

When he was in seventh grade, Roger made his school's football team. "He's got the mind and the arm to be a passer," his coach told his parents, "but he wants to be a halfback so he can run with the ball."

Roger attended Purcell High, a Catholic school for boys. In his senior year he stood 6'2" and weighed a sinewy 190 pounds. Until then he had played only a few minutes for the varsity. The Purcell coach liked to play only seniors.

In 1959, now a senior, Roger started for Purcell as quarterback. He still liked to run instead of pass. Once, in a huddle, he called for a run by the halfback. As the team trotted to the line of scrimmage, Roger said to the halfback: "Don't take the ball when I put it in your hands—I'm going to keep it."

The halfback stared, surprised. But he didn't take the ball. He dashed empty-handed into the line where tacklers pounced on him. They arose, triumphant. Then, jaws dropping, they watched Roger skirt the end, ball in hand, for a touchdown.

The delighted coach told Roger to run as often as he liked. Roger ducked, dodged, weaved, and wiggled through the flailing arms of tacklers. "Tackling Staubach," an opponent said, "is like trying to tackle the wind."

Purcell was among the best in the state of Ohio that 1959 season. Roger was picked on all-state teams. His teammates were happy for him. "I never met anyone who disliked Roger," halfback Vince Eysoldt said. "He is down-to-earth. He never gloats over anything."

Roger wanted to play for his favorite college team—Notre Dame. But a Notre Dame coach told him, "You are not a good enough passer to be our starting quarterback."

A Navy coach came to Cincinnati. He told Roger, "You are good enough to win the Heisman Trophy. And if you come to Navy, you will have a rewarding career as an officer in the United States Navy."

Roger promised to go to Navy. A few weeks later he played in a high school all-star game and was picked as the game's most valuable player. The Notre Dame coach phoned Roger and said, "We were wrong. You can be our number one quarterback. We will give you a free four-year scholarship."

"I'm sorry, sir," Roger said. "But I have promised to go to Navy." To Roger, a promise was a promise.

At Purcell, Roger had been a B student. He was president of the student council. But he had never done well in English grammar. When he took the test to be a Midshipman at the Naval Academy, he sailed by the math and science questions, but he stumbled over the grammar section and flunked the test.

The Navy sent him to a school in New Mexico to improve his grammar. He took the test again and passed. In the fall of 1961, Roger walked through the gates of the Naval Academy in Annapolis, Maryland, a plebe midshipman.

He wrote home most every night—to his parents and to Marianne Hoobler. She had been his classmate from the first to eighth grades. Now they were going steady.

In 1961, Roger played for a plebe team that didn't lose a game. In 1962, he made the jump to the varsity as its number one quarterback. In his first full game he ran and passed for 182 yards as Navy beat Boston College, 26–6. And a Navy coach reminded Roger of a prediction made three years earlier—that one day he would win the Heisman.

The 1962 team was young and made lots of mistakes. But it won five of its first nine games. Then came the game—Army. All week long Roger had been reminded of how important this game was to the Midshipmen and to Navy officers around the globe. Everywhere on campus there were signs that made the same demand—*Beat Army!*

Navy led, 15–6. The Midshipmen were chanting for another touchdown that would clinch the victory and make this year *their* year. But their quarterback, looking for an open receiver, was being wrestled to the ground by an Army tackler.

Roger whirled his body like a top. The tackler lost his grip on Roger's arm. Roger ran to his right. He looked toward the left sideline. He had sent two receivers down that left sideline to catch the attention of Army's defenders and swing them to the left.

Where was the open man on the right?

Roger heard a teammate yell, "Look out!" An Army tackler was bearing down on Roger. At that moment, he saw the flash of a white Navy jersey on his right. The tackler knifed through the air. Roger threw toward that flash of white. As the tackler slammed into his chest, pain flared through Roger's body. He went down hard, his helmeted head slamming against the turf.

And as he hit, he heard the crowd's loud roar.

Navy's Nick Markoff had grabbed the spiraling ball, no Army man near him. He sprinted 60 yards down the right sideline for a touchdown. Midshipmen tossed white caps high into the air. And they sang, "Sink the Army, sink the Army . . ."

Army had been sunk. Navy won, 34–14. Midshipmen carted Roger, his chest still aching, off the field on their shoulders. Into the Navy dressing room strode a former Navy lieutenant—President John F. Kennedy. "That Staubach," the president told coach Wayne Hardin, "he's amazing."

By the next season, 1963, much of the nation was saying the same thing about Roger the Dodger. In a game against Duke, Roger was hit by two Blue Devils.

Roger, as a Cowboy, does some scrambling.

As he toppled backward, he whipped the ball some 50 yards downfield. A Navy end settled under the spiral for a touchdown.

"His dodging gives us time to run away from defenders trying to cover us," one of his pass catchers, John Sai, told me in 1963. "As Roger dodges, he watches us. When one of us springs open while he's dodging, he tosses the ball for a long gain or a touchdown."

"When Roger is scrambling," coach Hardin said, "nobody knows what he is going to do except God and Roger Staubauch."

Between football games, however, all-American Roger was just another midshipman. He marched in formations. He snapped salutes. He pored over textbooks. He memorized the poems of Tennyson and stared at engineering charts. A Navy officer had to know a lot more than how to steer a battleship.

Most midshipmen awoke each morning at 6:15 as bells clanged. By then Roger had been up for more than

54

an hour. Almost every morning he attended Catholic mass.

Navy lost only one game (to SMU) that 1963 season. The Midshipmen beat Army in a game dedicated to their dead Commander in Chief, President Kennedy. He had been slain by an assassin only days earlier. Navy was ranked number two in the nation. Number one was the University of Texas. The two teams would clash in the Cotton Bowl on New Year's Day to decide who was number one.

First, however, Roger went to New York. A Navy coach's prediction had hit the bullseye. Roger accepted the Heisman Trophy as 1963's best football player. He was the second Navy player to win—the first being fullback Joe Bellino in 1960. He was only the second quarterback to win since Paul Hornung in 1956. Halfback John David Crow of Texas A & M won in 1957, halfback Pete Dawkins of Army in 1958, halfback Billy Cannon of Louisiana State in 1959, Bellino in 1960, halfback Ernie Davis of Syracuse in 1961 (he died of leukemia only a year later), and quarterback Terry Baker of Oregon State in 1962.

Roger's father spoke to the press at the Downtown Athletic Club. "I'll make it short," Edward Staubach told reporters. "We had only one child. The good Lord gave us a good one."

In the Cotton Bowl a few weeks later, a huge Texas line was spearheaded by tackle Scott Appleton. The Texas linemen buried Roger on play after play. Texas won easily, 28–6. After the game Roger said, smiling, "Now it's only God, Roger Staubach, and Scott Appleton who know what I am going to do next."

Would Roger, a junior, be the first to win the Heisman two years running? Roger heard the talk. He felt the pressure to have another astonishing season. Early in the 1964 season, however, he was hurt. He limped for much of the season, not able to dodge. Navy won only

Midshipman Staubach receives his Heisman from New York mayor Robert Wagner.

three of nine games. Another quarterback, Notre Dame's John Huarte, won the Heisman.

Pro teams were anxious to sign Roger after he graduated in June of 1965. Roger had promised the Navy he would serve four years after graduating. But he could resign from the academy before being commissioned as an officer.

In the spring of 1965, I asked Roger during a visit to the academy: "Will you turn pro?" A few weeks earlier Joe Namath, an Alabama quarterback, had signed a pro contract for more than $100,000 a season. As a Navy ensign, Roger would be paid about $5,000 a year.

"I am going to serve the four years I promised the Navy I would serve," Roger told me. I wondered if he would. The Staubach family was not wealthy. Roger's father had been in the hospital. Bills were piling up. Roger and Marianne planned to marry and newlyweds need money.

The Dallas Cowboys waved thousand dollar bills in front of Roger. But he said no when they offered him a pro contract. He put on his Navy ensign's uniform and went off to sea. To Roger, a promise was still a promise.

Four years later, the promise kept, he left the Navy to try to make the Cowboys as a quarterback. He was twenty-seven. People said he was too old to be an NFL rookie quarterback. He became one of the two or three greatest pro quarterbacks of the 1970s. And still the artful dodger, he was also one of pro football's trickiest runners. The Cowboys went to three Super Bowls with Roger throwing and running. They won twice.

In 1980, he retired. He didn't want to leave Dallas, where he was idolized. He became the owner of a company that bought and sold real estate. Roger's office was one of the rooms in the house where he and Marianne had raised their five children. In the summer of 1985, when a reporter came to visit him and Marianne, the reporter saw Roger playing basketball on a large court that Roger had built outside the house. The other players were former Cowboys and some of Roger's business friends. "We play a game almost every Saturday," Roger said. At 6'2" and about 195 pounds, he looked as fit as he had as a Cowboy quarterback.

What visitors to Roger's home rarely saw was his Heisman and other trophies. "He doesn't like to show off what he has won," his mother once said. "He feels that any talent comes from God, and so it isn't all your honor and glory."

Later a friend said, "You know, even when honor and glory came toward Roger, he dodged."

6

O. J. Simpson

THE SPARROW WHO
BECAME AN EAGLE

"The Cardiac Kids are trying to win another close one!"
the TV announcer shouted into the microphone. "But
this time the kids have a long, long way to go."

They had 94 yards to go. The Cardiac Kids were the
1968 University of Southern California football team.
They were called the Cardiac Kids because they often
won games in the last few seconds—as their fans'
hearts beat wildly.

The Cardiac Kids seemed unlikely to win this heart
thumper. USC and Washington were tied, 7–7. There
were fewer than three minutes left to play. The ball sat
on the USC 6, 94 yards from a touchdown. A tie seemed
certain.

USC's Trojans gathered in a huddle. The rangy 6',
200-pound running back, O. J. Simpson, stared at
quarterback Steve Sogge. "We can make those yards!"
O. J. shouted, banging a large fist into his palm. "It's
not too hard!"

Nothing ever seemed too hard for Juice, as his
friends called O. J. "I have always thought I could do
anything," he once told me when I was writing a book

about him. When he was thirteen, he sat in a San Francisco stadium and watched Jim Brown, then football's best runner, carry the ball for the Cleveland Browns. Jim Brown set dozens of rushing records.

After the game, O. J. stood with other teenagers outside the stadium. Jim Brown walked out. Boys screeched for his autograph. O. J. stared coolly at the huge hero. In a challenging voice he said, "One day I'll break all your records."

Brown smiled at the cocky teenager. He walked away without even asking what the name of the future record holder might be.

O. J. got his name from his aunt. When O. J. was born in San Francisco on July 9, 1947, his aunt suggested to his mother that he be named Orenthal "after a famous French movie actor." His mother wanted to name him James, after his father.

"Orenthal James!" shouted the aunt. "That's beautiful!"

Orenthal James twisted the tongues of the boy's pals when they tried to say it. They called him O. J. And from O. J. came Orange Juice or just plain Juice.

O. J. was sickly as a youngster. His mother and father had divorced. Eunice Simpson worked twelve hours a day washing and cleaning in a hospital. But sometimes there wasn't enough money for groceries to feed her three children. O. J. didn't drink enough milk. He had rickets, a disease which makes the bones fragile. He tried to make a Pop Warner football team when he was twelve. A coach told him to go home—he was too weak. Other boys laughed at him because his head seemed so large on his spindly body. "Your head's bigger than the rest of you," they jeered.

When O. J. was thirteen, Eunice got a better job. She bought bags of groceries for her children. "Look at that boy eat!" she exclaimed happily as O. J. wolfed down food. Until then he had been as thin as a sparrow. Now the sparrow began to fill out into an eagle.

And could that eagle fly! Running on his pipe-like legs, O. J. was the fastest boy in the neighborhood of housing projects. It was called Potrero Hill. O. J .had to be fast. Sometimes he was chased by the cops. O. J. and his pals stole food from stores. They ran down the back alleys of Potrero Hill and hid from angry merchants or police officers. Some of O. J.'s pals were caught. A few went to jail. "I was lucky," O. J. told me. "I nearly always got away."

On dusty lots, the boys played baseball, basketball, and football. "I was always the best at everything by the time I was fourteen or so," O. J. said. "And I was always a big enough loudmouth to go around telling everyone how good I was. I told myself, 'One day I am going to be as great as Willie Mays or Jim Brown. One day I am going to be *somebody.*' Many people think that young men in a black ghetto want only money. All I have ever wanted was to be *known,* to be famous, to be somebody."

At sixteen, O. J. was well known at Galileo High School. He was the school's best runner with a football. He was the longest hitter on the baseball team. He ran faster than anybody on the track team.

The trouble was, he was slower than anybody in opening a book. His teachers told him he had to study. "If you don't get good grades," they warned him, "no college will take you. Then you won't play college football and get the chance to break Jim Brown's records."

O. J. nodded. Two minutes later he dropped his books and streaked to the nearest ball game. "Not studying," he told me, "that was one of the two big mistakes I made."

The second mistake was stealing. The police came to Potrero Hill one day and arrested O. J. A store owner said he was one of several boys who had snatched bottles of wine. "I wasn't one of the guys who stole the wine," O. J. told me. "I stole a lot of things that I should have been arrested for. But the one time I was arrested, I hadn't done anything."

O. J. was locked overnight in a detention home. A judge freed him the next day. Never again, O. J. told himself, would he steal. He didn't want ever to be locked up again.

At seventeen, O. J. could brag—and he did—about a scrapbook filled with newspaper clippings. Newspaper articles told how he had scored more touchdowns than anyone in the history of Galileo High. He had taken one step down the road toward a place called Fame. But if he was going to be as famous as Jim Brown, he would have to set records as a college football player. And no college wanted him. His grades were too low.

In 1965, now eighteen, O. J. decided to enlist in the army. He knew he would likely be sent to fight in the jungles of Vietnam. There he might win medals and come home a famous hero.

The day before he was to enlist, he met a high school pal. The pal was playing on the football team at San Francisco's City College.

"Is your team any good?" O. J. asked.

"Too good for you to make," the pal answered, teasing.

Not good enough! O. J. thought he was good enough to do anything. His eyes flashed. "I bet I can make your team," he growled. He visited City College. His grades, said an official, were just good enough for a two-year junior college like City. He enrolled and a week later made the football team, winning the bet.

In the 1965 and 1966 seasons, O. J. scored at the rate of two touchdowns a game. He gained more yards than any junior-college player in history. City won seventeen of twenty games. O. J. was picked on a Junior College all-America. At last—a small measure of fame.

He studied. He read more books in two years than he had read in the previous ten. His grades were good enough for a senior college. A University of Southern California coach asked him if he would like to play his final two years of college football with the Trojans. O. J. knew that the Trojans went often to the Rose Bowl, the New Year's Day game watched by millions on TV. All of America could watch him flash over a football field. A delighted O. J. said, "I'm coming."

In 1967, he blurred through lines with the speed of a halfback and the bullish strength of a fullback. He dashed straight ahead as tacklers bounced off his massive thighs. He ran for the sidelines, running away from even the quickest tacklers. "You jam up your middle to stop him inside and he runs around you," an opposing coach said. "You spread out to stop him from going outside, he goes right through you like a knife into butter."

He gained more yards than any college back in the nation during that season. USC won the 1967 national championship by beating Indiana, 14—3, in the Rose Bowl. Now every football fan in the nation knew of Juice.

At first, O. J. wasn't disappointed to learn that UCLA quarterback Gary Beban had won the 1967 Heisman, the second quarterback in a row to win. (Florida's Steve Spurrier had won in 1966.) "Gary's been playing major college football for three years," O. J. said. "This was my first season. I'm not disappointed."

A few weeks later, however, he saw the Heisman Trophy for the first time, in the home of Mike Garrett, a former USC runner, who had won it in 1965. "It hit me kind of hard," O. J. said later. "For the first time I was aware how close I had come to winning, second to Gary in the voting. Now I knew how badly I wanted to win it in 1968."

That would be his senior year; his last chance to win the Heisman. Midway through the 1968 season the USC Cardiac Kids were again the nation's number one team. But in this game against Washington they were tied, 7–7. They had to go 94 yards to win and stay number one.

The Kids broke out of the huddle. Quarterback Steve Sogge took the snap, spun, and gave the ball to O. J. The Juice whirled, breaking away from tacklers. "He's as strong as a wrestler and as slippery as an eel," a Washington lineman later said. Juice stomped 14 yards to the 20 before he was brought down.

On play after play Sogge gave the ball to his work-horse. Bulling up the middle or squirting around the ends, O. J. carried the ball to the Washington 9-yard line. But now the clock blinked off the game's final minute.

"I'll get the touchdown right away, I promise," O. J. said. "Please let me try one more time."

Sogge gave it to him one more time. O. J. dashed into the gang-fight at the line of scrimmage. Pads cracked against helmets, O. J. saw an opening between colliding bodies. He dashed through the opening—"running for daylight," as the players say. Tacklers spun off him. He whirled into the end zone for the winning touchdown.

In the spotlight at last, O. J. has a firmer grasp on the Heisman than most tacklers ever had on him.

64

Tacklers strewn in his wake, O. J. drives for the yardage that broke pro football records.

In that 1968 season, O. J. gained more yards than any college back in history—1,880. He scored 23 touchdowns, an average of more than two a game. Late in November, he got a call from New York. He had won the trophy that now meant so much to him—the Heisman.

O. J. called his mother. He told her that she would come with him to New York, all her expenses paid. She would see her one-time sparrow receive college football's highest honor. As Juice talked to Eunice Simpson, who had worked so hard to make him strong, tears ran down his face.

In 1969, O. J. signed to play for the NFL's Buffalo Bills for more than $150,000 a year, the most any rookie had ever been paid. In 1972, he became the first runner to gain 2,000 yards in a season. True to his promise as a teenager, he had begun to break Jim Brown's records.

He never broke all of them. But when he retired in 1979, he was acclaimed the greatest runner of the 1970s and perhaps of all time.

O. J. in front of a mike, still where he likes to be—in the spotlight.

As jumpy off the field as he was carrying a football, O. J. always wanted to be busy. He became an actor in the movies. He talked a mile a minute on TV commercials for Hertz rental cars. That big bobbing head was seen in front of TV cameras at pro football and other sports events. Actor, salesman, TV sportscaster—O. J. wanted to do it all.

In 1985, he was living in Beverly Hills, near Hollywood, a neighborhood of movie stars. Seldom, however, did he get to sleep inside his mansion. Usually he was flying somewhere to be a telecaster at football games or to act in TV commercials and movies. "My home," he once told me, pointing up to the sky, "is an iron bird up there."

That iron bird carried a very rich man. More important to O. J., it carried an Orenthal James Simpson who had indeed become a *somebody*.

7

Jim Plunkett

THE PACT AND THE DREAM

He put down the phone slowly. Twenty-two-year-old Jim
Plunkett could hardly believe what he had just heard.
All he had to do was sign his name on a contract and
he'd be earning $100,000 a year. *A hundred thousand
dollars a year!* Just three years earlier, Jim had been
pumping gas at midnight for a dollar an hour. He had
never made more than $4,000 a year in his life. *A
hundred thousand dollars a year!* He and his sisters
had worked day and night to help support their mother
and father, both of whom were blind. *A hundred
thousand dollars a year!*

*Yes, but what about the dream? And what about
the pledge to beat USC?*

A year earlier, in 1969, Jim's Stanford team had lost
to USC, 26–24. A Trojan kicker had booted the winning
field goal just as the gun sounded to end the game.

A dejected Jim trudged to the dressing room with his
close pal, pint-sized receiver Randy Vataha. "We'll beat
Southern California next year," Randy said.

"I promise it," Jim said. Minutes later he and his
teammates shook hands on a secret pact—next year
they would beat USC.

Then Jim told them about his dream that he had so often—that Stanford's Indians rode into the Rose Bowl on New Year's Day and won.

Jim couldn't go to the Rose Bowl if he took that $100,000, nor could he make good on the pact to beat USC. He'd be a pro, playing for a team in the National Football League.

Jim could turn pro because he had not played as a freshman in 1966. His class was graduating in June, 1970. According to the college rules, Jim could stay for one more season of college football in the fall. Or he could turn pro and make all that money.

And how could somebody turn his back on all that money?

Certainly he'd never had much money. He was born in the bustling city of San Jose, California, on December 5, 1947. He was the third child—and only son—of Carmen and William Plunkett. William Plunkett had been born with poor vision and could not see at all by the time he was twenty-five. Carmen had been stricken by a disease that blinded her when she was twenty. The two had met at a New Mexico school for the blind and married.

There were not many jobs for blind men and women in San Jose. William Plunkett sold newspapers from behind a counter in the San Jose post office. Carmen took odd jobs. Of Mexican descent, they spoke Spanish to each other, but English to their children. Since neither Jim nor his sisters spoke a word of Spanish, they could not understand when their parents talked to each other.

"My dad couldn't bring in much money," Jim once said. "So it was expected that as soon as we could, my sisters and I would get jobs." After school twelve-year-old Jim pumped gas. On weekends he delivered newspapers from door to door.

"My folks were poor and uneducated," he once told me, "but they didn't complain. They accepted what was good in their lives and what was bad. For me and my sisters, our lives were pretty much the same as those of our friends. No one in the neighborhood had much money. The only difference for us was that because both our parents were blind, we had to stay around the house a lot to make sure they were all right."

When he had the time to play on weekends, Jim threw baseballs faster than anyone in the neighborhood. When he was fourteen, he heard about a football-throwing contest. Jim won by tossing a football 63 yards on the fly.

Always husky and tall, he stood 6'2" and weighed 200 pounds as a junior at James Lick High School. The Lick coach had heard about the football-throwing contest. He picked Jim as his quarterback. In two years, Jim's soaring passes helped James Lick win seventeen of eighteen games.

Notre Dame was among the dozens of colleges that wanted Jim. But the Notre Dame campus at South Bend, Indiana, was some 2,000 miles away from San Jose. Jim decided to stick close to his blind mother and father. He chose nearby Stanford University.

Stanford was known for two things. One, students had to study long hours to keep up with their work. Two, the Stanford football team usually lost more often than it won. The Indians hadn't won the Pacific-8 Conference championship, which meant a trip to the Rose Bowl on New Year's Day, in almost twenty years.

Jim felt strange during his freshman year, 1966, at Stanford. He worried about his grades. And he didn't know anybody. "I have always had trouble making new friends," he once said. "Other students looked down on football players. They called us The Animals." One evening, wandering alone on the campus and worrying about passing a troublesome test the next day, he told himself: "I don't belong here."

A few days later he was in a hospital. During a physical, a doctor discovered a small tumor on Jim's neck. The tumor was not dangerous, but it had to be removed. The surgery made him too weak to play football in 1966, making him eligible to play from 1967 to 1970. When Jim tried to throw footballs in practice, his spirals wobbled. He now had a new worry. Maybe he wasn't strong enough to be a college passer.

Broad-shouldered, with a mass of curly dark hair and melting brown eyes, Jim shied away from almost everyone on the campus. He spoke so softly that teachers had to ask him to speak louder. He began to think of himself as a failure in the classroom, a failure on the football field.

Then he became friendly with an implish, laughing pass catcher. Randy Vataha, who at 5'9" was among the smallest players on the team. He was so small that he could zip into a Mickey Mouse suit and be a prancing, joyful Mickey to visitors one summer at Disneyland in Anaheim, California. He also could zip away from taller pass defenders with sudden bursts of speed. Randy told people—there was nothing shy about Randy—that he could one day be a pro pass catcher.

Randy's bubbling joy infected Jim. Randy laughed and joked and did crazy things. His pal, Jim Plunkett, began to smile. Randy told Jim that he could be a great passer—and Jim began to believe him.

One day the football coach asked Jim to come to his office. The coach said he didn't think Jim could be the Stanford quarterback in 1967. "But you're big and strong. Next fall we will try you at defensive end."

"Give me a chance at quarterback," Jim pleaded. "Then decide."

The coach agreed. That fall a healthy, strong, and confident Jim spiraled passes of 60 and 70 yards. Two gluey-handed receivers, Randy and Bobby Moore, camped under those long tosses for touchdowns. By the end of the 1967 season, Jim had thrown for 2,156 yards—the most ever completed in one season by a Pacific-8 passer.

And he had only started. By his junior year he had racked up 4,829 yards in passing, more than any Pacific-8 passer ever. And Jim still had one more season to go.

In that 1969 season, USC edged the Indians with a field goal after the game had ended. Watching from the sideline, Jim had seen the ball curl between the posts. Later he said to Randy, "People are saying we can't win the close ones. Well, this is the last time this will happen. We just have to beat USC next time, we just *have* to."

He and the other players swore to each other solemnly: We will beat USC. But, in the spring of 1970, the other players were casting curious looks at Jim. Would he turn pro? His phone rang most every day. Which was more important to him? That $100,000 a year? Or a pact with his teammates to beat USC?

Jim thought about his teammates. They looked up to the brawny Number 16. One of his blockers told a reporter, "If a tackler ever got by me and hurt Jim, I would turn in my uniform."

Jim couldn't desert them. He said no to the offers of $100,000. He told a friend, "If I was to leave now, I would always have the feeling that I let them down before our goals were reached."

Jim had two goals—beating USC and winning in the Rose Bowl. Stanford hadn't beaten USC in thirteen

Jim shows the passing form that helped him to win the 1970 Heisman.

years, but Jim made victory over USC look easy. He completed nineteen passes for a total of 275 yards. The jubilant Indians carried him off the field 24—14 winners.

72

Now they had only to beat Washington State and UCLA to win the Pacific-8 title and go to the Rose Bowl. Early in the State game, the ball sat on the Indian 4-yard line. Jim told Randy to run as far and as fast as he could. Jim ducked into the end zone and hurled the ball. Randy steaked under the spiral, grabbed it, then kept on going. That 96-yard touchdown play was one of many. Stanford won, 63–16.

Next came the UCLA Bruins. Twice in that game, Jim told Randy to go deep. He soared passes that the little receiver pulled down for long gains. Those long passes put the Indians close enough to kick field goals and win, 9–7.

The Indians, at last, were going to the Rose Bowl. They faced Ohio State, which hadn't lost a game all season. Stanford had lost three, including its last two. The Buckeyes were picked to win by at least ten points.

Ohio State led by four, 17–13, as the fourth period began. And the Buckeyes stood only 20 yards away from another touchdown. But, on the 20, the Stanford defense held. Now it was up to the Stanford offense to get a go-ahead touchdown.

Into the game, running, came Jim, Randy Vataha, and Bobby Moore. "We can go these 80 yards for the touchdown that'll put us ahead," Jim told his offense. "We've done it before."

Jim knew that Ohio State had seen movies of the Washington State and UCLA games. They would be looking for those long passes to Vataha.

Jim called for short passes—to Vataha on the left, then to Moore on the right, then back to Vataha over the middle. Ohio State clamped two backs onto Moore, another two onto Vataha. That left holes in the Buckeye middle. Jim shot his running backs through that spaced-out middle.

In eleven plays, Stanford gulped short hunks of yardage from its own 20 to the Buckeye 39. Jim told

The quarterback of the Los Angeles Raiders in 1984, Jim points his troops in the right direction.

Randy to go short, Bobby to go long. He stepped back. He saw Randy knocked to the ground. He looked for Bobby. He couldn't find him. Two Buckeye tacklers knifed through the air, straight at him. Then, way downfield, Jim saw Bobby slant toward the goal line. Jim threw—and at that exact moment the two tacklers slammed him to the grass.

Buried under some 400 pounds of Buckeyes, Jim heard the crowd's roar. He jumped up. Bobby had leaped high at the 2-yard line to snatch the ball away from a Buckeye defender.

Jim rushed to the 2. From there he sent a ball carrier crashing over the goal line. Stanford led, 20–17. Minutes later, Jim lined another pass—a 10-yard bullet—that Randy snatched in the end zone. Stanford walked off the field 27–17 winners of the Rose Bowl. Jim shook hands with his teammates. A year-old pledge had been kept and a dream had come true.

Jim poses in the lobby of the Downtown Athletic Club with the original Heisman Trophy. His name would soon be added to the list of winners on the trophy's base.

In that 1970 season, there were dozens of outstanding quarterbacks, notably Notre Dame's Joe Theismann, Ohio State's Rex Kern, Mississippi's Archie Manning, and Auburn's Pat Sullivan. The easy winner of the Heisman was Stanford's Jim Plunkett. "I had a lot of good reasons for staying at school this past season," he told people at the Downtown Athletic Club. "There was USC, the Rose Bowl, and now the Heisman."

One statistic seemed to prove beyond much doubt that he was the best. He had finished as a college passer with 7,887 yards. That was more yardage than any player had gained during a career in 101 years of college football.

Jim and Randy Vataha went on to play for the New England Patriots. Later Jim joined the Oakland (now

Los Angeles) Raiders. His passing was a big reason why the Raiders won the Super Bowl in 1981 and again in 1984. Jim lived near Los Angeles where he often played in tennis tournaments. He liked to say he was a better tennis player than he was a football player—and, of course, no one believed him, least of all Jim Plunkett. A pass catcher named Randy Vataha had taught him a long time ago that the road to greatness begins with one large step—believing in yourself.

8

Archie Griffin

A TRICK AND A PRAYER

The streak was snapped. Archie Griffin didn't care that the streak was ending. At halftime, the burly senior told his friend, Buckeye quarterback Cornie Greene, "I'd give up the whole thirty-one-game streak and even my Heisman to win this one."

"This one" was a 1975 battle between Ohio State and Michigan. Both teams were unbeaten. Each was tied for the Big Ten championship. The winner would go to the Rose Bowl on New Year's Day.

Ohio State had gone to three straight Rose Bowls in Archie's freshman, sophomore, and junior seasons. The 5'9", 180-pound cannonball was determined to make it four in a row in this, his last regular-season game in an Ohio State uniform. As a junior in 1974, Archie had gained more yards than any running back in the nation. He had become only the fifth junior—the first since Roger Staubach—to win the Heisman. He had gained 100 or more yards in twenty-one straight games—a college record. If he could continue that streak through this 1975 season, he had a chance to become the first player to win the Heisman twice.

He had gained only 35 yards so far against a Michigan team that had ganged up on him. Two and even

Archie Griffin: Like a BB shot from a gun.

three tacklers struck him down whenever he touched the ball. Now there were fewer than eight minutes left. Michigan led, 14–7. The ball sat on the Ohio State 10, 90 yards from a tie. Ohio State hadn't been able to make a first down since the second period more than an hour ago. Ohio State could forget about a fourth straight Rose Bowl. Archie could forget about his streak and a second Heisman. Michigan had stopped cold both Ohio State and its star.

"Let's say a little prayer," Cornie Green said after the quarterback called a play in the Buckeye huddle. Cornie was always saying "Let's say a little prayer" when the Buckeyes were in trouble. But as Ohio State trotted to the line of scrimmage, Cornie knew he had more than a prayer going for him. He had a little trick up the sleeve of his jersey. "After all," as Cornie said later, "God helps those who help themselves."

* * *

James Griffin had taught his children well how to pray and how to help themselves. A Bible was always open in the living room of the small house in Columbus, Ohio, where Archie was born on August 24, 1954. Archie was one of six boys and a girl. Swearing, cursing, and smoking were strictly forbidden in the Griffin house. Hard work was encouraged.

James Griffin worked twenty hours almost every day. During the mornings and afternoons he drove a garbage truck and hoisted 100-pound cans into the truck. At night, he shoveled coal in a blazing-hot steel mill. Between those jobs, he mopped school floors as a janitor.

"It was very easy to get into trouble with your father not around," recalls James, Jr., the oldest Griffin boy. The Griffins lived in a neighborhood filled with toughs and delinquents not far from the Ohio State football stadium. "None of us ever got into trouble. That shows the respect we had for our father. He had a dream—that if you do your best, you will succeed regardless of color or class."

All the Griffin children helped their mother keep the house clean. When he was twelve, Archie delivered newspapers. Each Saturday he brought home his earnings, a dollar and a half, and gave them to his mother. Then he and the other boys ran off to a nearby lot that was strewn with broken glass and rocks. The lot, they imagined, was the Ohio State football field.

Two of the smallest Griffins, Archie and Ray, played on the same team. Ray was a typical Griffin—strong and fast. Archie waddled. He was the shortest Griffin boy. He was also the fattest. The other kids laughed when he walked. They called him Tank.

"I was too slow and too fat to catch and tackle anybody," Archie once said. "They put me in the middle of the line. I was so wide no one could run over me."

Then, Archie decided to slim down. He stopped eating the candy bars he relished. He lifted "weights"—actually cases of old bottles filled with sand. He'd always had slim legs. Soon those legs supported a muscled torso.

Thirteen-year-old Archie tried out for his junior high football team. He made the squad. His father went to watch his first game.

On the first play Archie ran 50 yards for a touchdown. The play was called back. Someone had been offside. On the next play Archie ran 55 yards for a touchdown. That, too, was called back. Another offside. On the next play Archie sped 60 yards for a touchdown. The panting officials didn't call that one back. In the stands, James Griffin said to a friend, pointing at his son, "We got something here."

No longer was Archie the family tank. Now he was the family thunderbolt. At Eastmoor High a coach said, "I can never remember one man tackling him. They had to bring a whole army to bury him."

First of all, Archie was fast—the fastest sprinter on the track team. Second, he was quick—he could shoot straight ahead, then flick left or right with a blinding-fast turn. Third, he was strong—so strong he knocked 200-pound tacklers backward with an upward lift of his weightlifter's shoulders. One tackler said, blinking, after being bowled over by Archie: "He's 180 pounds who hits like 280."

Ohio State coach Woody Hayes dearly loved fast and strong runners. Woody always liked to run instead of pass. "When you pass," he said, "three things can happen—a completion, an incompletion, or an interception. And two of the three are bad."

Woody wanted Archie and Archie wanted Ohio State. Then his father could slip away from one of his jobs in Columbus to see him play. "I always wanted to do my

Archie runs for daylight—and a record.

best when he came to see me play," Archie said. "Then he wouldn't have wasted his few hours away from work."

In Ohio State's first game of the 1972 season, against Iowa, the scared freshman ran into the game. He fumbled. Woody pulled him out of the game. Archie watched from the bench as the Buckeyes won, 21–0.

Before the next game, Archie prayed. "I asked the Lord to give me a chance to play," he said. "I read the Bible where it said, 'Knock, and the door shall be opened.'"

Coach Hayes kept the door shut. He feared that Archie might fumble again in the next game. Archie sat on the bench as North Carolina went ahead 7–0. Ohio State could not score. Finally, a desperate Woody waved Archie into the game.

The nervous Archie flew onto the field—then realized he had forgotten his helmet. He jammed on the helmet in the huddle as he thanked the Lord for opening the door.

Archie swept around end for 7. He plunged up the middle for 6. He bolted off-tackle and weaved 32 yards for a touchdown.

That day he gained 239 yards, an Ohio State record for one game. Archie gained 772 yards that season, a record for a freshman. Ohio State won nine of ten games and went to the Rose Bowl, losing 42–17 to USC even though Archie gained almost 5 yards a try.

In the 1973 season, Archie gained 129 yards in the opening game, a 56–7 rout of Minnesota. That began his streak of gaining at least 100 yards a game. By season's end, he had rushed for 1,428 yards. Ohio State was unbeaten, tied only by Michigan. Again the Buckeyes went to the Rose Bowl, this time routing USC, 42–21.

In 1974, Archie began his junior year with his eyes fixed on a record. The most yards ever gained by a college rusher was 4,715. By now Archie had 2,220—and he still had two seasons to play.

He also had the respect of his teammates—both for the way he was off the field and on the field. Buckeye quarterback Cornie Greene liked to wear green pants and cherry-red vests with his canary-yellow shoes. He laughed when he saw Archie dressed in a banker's grey suit and black shoes. But as Archie talked about why it was important to study and work hard and make a good impression, Cornie stopped laughing and began to listen.

"At first I was Flash and he was Class," Cornie said. "I'd watch Kojak on the TV while Archie was studying his books or reading the Bible."

Once Archie came into a dorm and saw Cornie and two other players. He knew they had cut their class. He told them they were wrong to cut classes.

"If it had been anyone else," Cornie said, "we would have thrown him out. But not Archie. We respect him too much. We all felt bad."

After that, Cornie began to go to all his classes. He read the Bible with Archie. "It got to working on me, you know," he said. "Pretty soon he made me receive Jesus Christ into my life."

In tight spots, Cornie began to tell the Buckeyes, "Let's say a little prayer." In the 1974 season, the Buckeyes won nine of ten. They lost only to Michigan State. Again they went to the Rose Bowl where, this time, USC eked out an 18–17 victory.

Archie yawned away from so many tacklers that he gained 1,620 yards, more than anyone in the nation. He stretched to twenty-one his streak of having gained at least 100 yards a game. He needed only a half-dozen more to break the record. He needed 895 yards to smash the record of 4,715 in a career.

"If anyone can, Archie will," said Coach Woody Hayes.

He wasn't talking about Archie breaking those two records. He was talking about Archie becoming the first to win the Heisman Trophy twice. After that 1974 season, Archie had been presented with the Heisman, the first junior to win it since Roger Staubach in 1963. Injuries had stopped Roger in 1964 and Doak Walker in 1949 when they tried to win the trophy a second time as seniors. As the 1975 season began, Archie was bombarded with the same question: "Do you think you will be the first to win the Heisman two years in a row?"

"I know I will be a marked man," Archie said. "I know every team will be out to stop me. But my favorite topic when I talk to kids is the Three D's—Determination, Dedication, and Desire. I think the Three D's will help me win the Heisman again."

Since 1970, when Jim Plunkett won, the winners had all been running backs with one exception. That was Auburn quarterback Pat Sullivan in 1971. Nebraska running back Johnny Rodgers won in 1972, Penn State runner John Cappelletti in 1973, Archie in 1974. "In 1975," Archie said with a smile, "I hope they go on picking running backs."

The Buckeyes roared through the first six games of the 1975 season, routing North Carolina 32–7, clobbering UCLA 41–20, and burying Wisconsin 56–0. Archie ran his streak to twenty-seven—a new record.

Ohio State met Purdue. Archie reeled away for runs of 25 and 30 yards. He had passed 4,700 yards in his career. He needed only 15 to become the runner with the most yards ever. A big crowd of almost 70,000 was standing, waiting to see the record smashed.

"Okay," Cornie Green said in the huddle. "Let's say a little prayer and get those yards." The ball was on the Purdue 39. Cornie took the snap, spun, and gave the ball to Archie, who veered toward the outside, following fullback Scott Dannelley.

A tackler spread wide his arms. "Get 'em!" Archie shouted. Scott leaped. His long body cut down the tackler. Archie twisted away from another tackler, then bowled over a third. He fought his way to the 15 where a safety caught him by the ankles and twisted him to the ground.

Archie rose, leaping. Teammates pounded him on the shoulders. The announcer told the cheering crowd that Archie's 24-yard run had set the record. Coach Hayes waved him off the field to bask in the applause.

Four Saturdays later, still unbeaten, the Buckeyes were losing to Michigan, 14–7. Their hopes of a fourth-straight Rose Bowl seemed to be flowing down a drain—only eight minutes left, 90 yards to go for a tie.

Archie's streak was ended at 31. The Wolverine line-backers had set their sights on him, two panting at his heels wherever he went, and so far Archie had gained only 35 yards.

But Coach Hayes had put a trick up Cornie Greene's sleeve. In the huddle Cornie told Archie: "I'll fake giving you the ball—don't take it."

The center snapped the ball to Cornie. He spun. Archie dashed forward. Two Michigan linebackers hurled themselves into the line to knock him down. They saw the ball float over their heads. Turning, they watched a Buckeye catch Cornie Green's pass for a 15-yard again.

Now—*was it too late?*—Ohio State had a way of fooling those linebackers. If Cornie wanted to throw to his left, he sent Archie into the left side. Linebackers, thinking he had the ball, rushed up. The left flank was open. Into the left flank dashed a Buckeye to catch a pass from Cornie.

Three straight passes to the left and right leap-frogged the Buckeyes into Michigan territory. Cornie guessed that the linebackers would drop back, expecting a pass. Cornie gave the ball to Archie, who whisked by the confused defenders for an 11-yard gain. On the next play, the linebackers rushed up, anxious to stop another charge by Archie. Cornie faked giving the ball to Archie, kept it, and shot by the defenders for a 12-yard gain to the Michigan 5. From there fullback Pete Johnson slashed his way into the end zone. Michigan 14, Ohio State 14.

Then Michigan made a mistake. Eager to score quickly, the Michigan quarterback tossed a wild pass. Playing on defense for Ohio State was Ray Griffin, Archie's speedy brother. Ray plucked down the pass and fought his way to the 2. Again Pete Johnson plunged over for a second Ohio State touchdown

With club officials, Archie stands with the Heisman in 1974, his first of two.

within three minutes. Ohio State won, 21–14. Coach Hayes called the game "our greatest comeback in twenty-five years."

Ohio State went to the Rose Bowl for a fourth straight year. This time they lost to UCLA, 23-14. For the third straight year Archie was on most all-American teams. His name went into the record books for having gained the most yards in a career—5,177—and the most consecutive games in which he gained 100 yards—31. When the voting for the Heisman was announced, Archie became the first to win it twice.

Archie also became the first Heisman winner to graduate ahead of his class. He earned a degree in industrial management and then signed to play pro football for the Cincinnati Bengals. In seven seasons as a Bengal, he gained an average of 4 yards a carry even though, at 5'9" and about 190 pounds, he was among the smallest runners in the NFL.

In 1985, he said good-bye to football. He went back to Columbus and became a highly paid executive. By now his football salary had made him at least half a millionaire. But, as he said, "I'm like my dad—I believe hard work will keep anyone out of trouble. An idle mind is indeed the devil's workshop."

Like his father, Archie was never idle on or off a football field. But who would expect idleness from the first man in the world who could say that he had enough Heisman Trophies for bookends?

9

Tony Dorsett

A RIDE ON THE NOSE
OF A FOOTBALL

His left elbow was jammed. When he touched it, he winced with pain. His right eye was swollen half-shut and what you could see of the eye was bloodshot. A 200-pounder's helmet had crashed into his left thigh. He limped as he came back onto the field. The game was only fifteen minutes old.

This was the 1976 blood match between the University of Pittsburgh and the University of Syracuse. Before the game the Syracuse Orangemen had a single battle cry—"Stop Number 33." Number 33 was Pittsburgh's Tony Dorsett. T. D., as his teammates called him because of his initials, had gained more yards than any college runner in history. He had shattered Archie Griffin's year-old record of 5,177. With half a season left, Tony had set his sights on a peak never before attained—6,000 yards.

So far, he hadn't netted even one yard. In fact, Syracuse tacklers had bounced him backward for a total loss of five yards.

"Stop Number 33 and you beat Pitt!"

That's what Syracuse defenders told each other before the game. So far they had been proven right. They had stopped Tony dead in his tracks. They knocked him out of the game for a while as doctors fixed his jammed elbow. Now he was half-blind, aching, and limping. And Syracuse led, 7–3.

Pitt players stared at the beat-up Tony. They told him to stay on the bench. "No," he said, walking gingerly onto the field for the start of the second quarter. "I'm staying in. This is going to be a dogfight."

Being beat up on a football field was better than sweating and straining in a steel mill back in Aliquippa. Tony often told that to people when they marveled how his 5′10″, 160-pound body could take the beatings from 250-pound tacklers. See a steel mill once, you remember it—the shimmering heat, the screech of metal, the sweating bodies of the men hurling coal into huge blast furnaces.

He had been a boy, only twelve, his eyes bulging, on that morning when he stared at the heat and heard the noise. His father worked here in the mill. He had brought Tony to show him what a mill was like. "If you don't get an education," he told the boy, "you'll end up here."

Tony gulped. He didn't ever want to see the hellish scene again. As soon as he could, he told himself, he was going to fly out of Aliquippa, maybe on the nose of a football.

Tony was born in Aliquippa, which is near Pittsburgh, on April 7, 1954. His parents lived in a run-down section of town. Gangs roamed the back alleys. They hurled bottles and swung bats at each other. Tony was the smallest in his gang. His saucer-like eyes looked so big that other kids called him Hawk Eyes.

When gang fights started, little Tony took off. "I was too scared to fight those big guys," he once told me. "That's how I think I got so fast—running away from those bloody fights."

He grew bigger, stronger, and more than a little meaner. By his junior year at Hopewell High, Tony stood a compactly-muscled 5′10″ and weighed 160 pounds. Other kids were more respectful now that he had muscles. They called him Hawk.

The Hawk flew away from tacklers. On the basketball court he moved so fast that opponents called him, "Now You See Him, Now You Don't." Tony had a goal. "I told myself," he later said, "that I would decide on one sport—football or basketball—and whichever one I picked, I would be known as number one."

Eager to be number one, he sometimes knocked people out of the way to get there. In several basketball games he traded punches with bigger opponents. No longer did he dread fighting—he was getting to like it. But after one fistfight, his coach told Tony: "One more fight and I'll toss you off the team."

Tony had a talk with himself. If he was going to fly out of Aliquippa, if he was going to be number one in basketball or football, he had to stay on the team. He had to obey the rules.

"After that I calmed down," he told me. "I didn't jump at people over small things. I decided to keep my fighting limited to running over people."

Tony saved all the energy of his rages until he ran with a football. A one-time Army football player had Tony's violent temper. He too held in his anger until he could knock over people on a gridiron or smack a ball over a fence in baseball games. He loved team sports and later coached teams. Even later he was a World War II general and the President of the United States— Dwight David Eisenhower.

By 1972, Tony's senior year at Hopewell High, he had run over so many people that he was scoring an average of two touchdowns a game. One magazine said he was the number one high school player in the nation.

That made up Tony's mind—his sport would be football. And one day, he told himself, he would be the number one college football player.

He chose a school whose football team was perhaps number one hundred in the country. The University of Pittsburgh team had lost ten of eleven games in the 1972 season. Tony could have gone to USC, which had won all twelve of its games for the national championship. But California was too far from Aliquippa. He didn't want to be so far from his family.

To a wide-eyed Tony, the spawling University of Pittsburgh campus seemed like a city in itself. He knew nobody. He felt lost and scared in the crowds of students rushing toward classes.

One night he phoned his mother. He told her he was leaving the campus and coming home. His mother said, "Remember, you will only once get this chance for a college education."

Tony hung up. He thought about what she had said. If he went back to Aliquippa without a college degree, he'd have to go to work in the steel mill. And what about all his cocky talk about being number one in football? He'd hear lots of jeers in Aliquippa.

Tony made himself walk with confidence through the campus crowds. He smiled at strange faces. To his surprise, people smiled back and said hello. Others were also anxious to make friends.

On Saturday afternoons he heard cheers, then roars from spectators as he ran away from tacklers like a BB shot from a gun. "He is the fastest running back who ever played this game," Army coach Homer Smith said. When tacklers trapped Tony, he shifted, spun, wiggled, twisted and somehow, as often as not, broke away. That 1973 season he gained 1,586 yards—the most by any freshman ever. And the Panthers won six of their twelve games. From the worst one hundred they jumped to the top fifty.

In 1974, Tony gained more than a thousand yards and broke the school's thirty-five year record for rushing. And Hawk still had two more seasons to go. His wide eyes were now fixed on an Ohio State junior, Archie Griffin, who was streaking toward a career record of 5,177 yards. In 1975, his junior year, Tony galloped for 1,500 yards to come within about 1,000 yards of the record.

"Tony is quicker than a hiccup and tougher than week-old bread," a Panther coach said early in the 1976 season. The toughness came after months of lifting weights. His 5'10" frame now weighed a hefty 190 pounds. The Hawk had the build and size of a heavy-weight boxer.

All his life he had yearned to be number one in his sport. Now he was close, within a thousand yards of being the greatest ground gainer ever. And his team was just as close to being number one. In pre-season forecasts for the 1976 season, Pitt was picked among the top ten.

"Number 33 is going to have to turn it on even if he is hurting," Panther coach Johnny Majors told an assistant. Syracuse led, 7–3, in the second period. The Orangemen had steeled themselves to stop Pitt, ranked number one in the nation midway through the 1976 season. And to stop Pitt, the Orangemen had to stop Tony. For fifteen minutes they had stopped him for a loss of 5 yards.

Tony stared with one bleary, half-shut eye at the Orangemen. This, indeed, was a dogfight. So far he

Tony Dorsett shows the flying feet that propelled him to a rushing record as a Pitt Panther. The Panthers, as a result, rose to become the nation's number one team.

had gotten the worst of the fighting—swollen eye, aching elbow, a leg that limped. He could't run with his usual speed—and, maybe, that might be a way to fool the Orangemen.

Tony took the ball and ran to the right at only half-speed. Two tacklers veered toward him. Tony suddenly

Tony lopes into the end zone, an official raising his hands to signal a touchdown. By the end of his career at Pitt, Tony's initials meant more than Tony Dorsett.

picked up speed. The tacklers hesitated, then lunged—too late. Tony looped around them, then ran gimpy-legged 33 yards into Syracuse territory. Minutes later he plunged over for a touchdown and Pitt led, 10–7.

Syracuse fought back. Late in the game the Orangemen led, 13–10. Tony's left arm hurt so badly that he couldn't straighten it. The Pitt quarterback asked him if he could hold onto a ball pitched to him. Tony nodded. The Pitt quarterback knew that Syracuse, seeing Tony's crippled arm, would not expect him to try to catch a pass.

The ball was 33 yards away from a Pitt touchdown. The Pitt quarterback took the snap, wheeled, and pitched the ball to Tony as he ran toward the sideline. Tony grimaced as the ball smacked into his hands, the left arm as straight as he could make it. He swept around the Syracuse flank. No one had expected to see

94

Tony—so far from the ball—suddenly carrying it. Tony ran down the sideline. A safetyman—the last Orangeman between him and the goal—saw Tony's limp. He knew Tony couldn't outrun him.

The safetyman angled to the sideline. There he could trap Tony and knock him out of bounds.

Tony knew he couldn't outrun the safetyman on his sore leg. He spun—and, as the crowd gasped, he ran straight at the safetyman.

The surprised safety had been going one way. Now he had to go another. He stumbled, off-balance, as Tony came within an arm's length. The safety reached out an arm. Tony whacked it away and then loped to the end zone with the winning touchdown.

The Panthers won all twelve games that 1976 season. They beat Georgia in the Sugar Bowl to be acclaimed number one in the nation. Tony gained 1,948 yards for the season to break Archie Griffin's career record and set a new one—6,082. He tied Glenn Davis's thirty-year-old record of 59 touchdowns and broke Davis's record of 354 points by scoring 356. Now, T.D. meant more than Tony Dorsett.

Tony began to wear a gold medal around his neck. On the medal was engraved the number 1. The medal told Tony and the world that the Hawk had reached his goal of being the best and playing for the best. He wore the medal to New York to accept another symbol of the best—the Heisman.

"Ever since I made all-American as a freshman," Tony told people, "this trophy has been what I wanted most. It recognizes me as the best."

"You are the best runner ever," an interviewer said.

Never shy about telling people he was number one, Tony said quickly, "I think my statistics prove it."

Tony joined the Dallas Cowboys. He became their top runner and certainly one of the two or three best in the

NFL during the late 1970s and early 1980s. The Cowboys gave their number one something else he had always wanted—what he called "the mean green." That was money.

The Cowboys signed Tony to a contract worth about one million dollars over five years. Tony bought an $80,000 home for his parents. He bought himself a millionaire's palatial home in a posh Dallas suburb. He bought sleek sports cars and fast motorcycles.

He also listened to bad advice. People told him to invest money so he could save money by paying smaller income-tax bills. He lost over a million dollars in those investments. His Cowboy teammates were sympathetic. Said quarterback Randy White: "By the time an athlete learns how to invest, it's too late."

Tony had learned. "Now, when I want advice on how to invest," he said in 1985, "I listen mainly to myself."

This makes sense coming from someone who had listened to himself back in Aliquippa, deciding that one day he could fly away from the horrors of a steel mill on the nose of a football. On that flight he had soared to a record and a Heisman, heights that might dizzy others but not a hawk.

10

Earl Campbell

PRIDE AND LOVE

The fat man limped into the room. He sat down on a cot. He winced as he grabbed his sore leg.

His roommate stared at him. A year earlier, the fat man with the sore leg had been an all-American running back here at the University of Texas. He had rammed through opposing lines—a 5'11", 220-pound fire hydrant of muscle. Now, sitting on the cot with a grimace on his face, Earl Campbell was a 260-pound barrel of fat.

"I ought to quit football," Earl said to his roommate. "I'm no good to the team, no good to myself."

Two years earlier, as a freshman, Earl Campbell had two dreams. The first: that he would lead the nation in rushing yardage by his senior year. The second: that he would win the Heisman.

His roommate reminded him of his yearning for the Heisman.

"No way I can win the Heisman," Earl growled, "when I can't even walk."

Not being able to walk, sitting on the bench for almost half this 1976 season, Earl had watched his body balloon. Overweight, out of shape, leg aching, what good was he to the Longhorn football team?

No good at all.

But once before he had thought he was no good to himself or to his mother—and then look what happened.

Earl Christian Campbell was born on March 29, 1955, in a shack made of old planks. Its buckled front door was painted a sickly green, its walls cracked and the paint peeling, holes in the roof. Earl and his ten brothers and sisters went to sleep at night staring up at the stars. They awoke shivering under thin blankets.

The house sat on a small farm. A blacktopped road curled by it and snaked up and down hills into Tyler, a small town in east Texas. Earl's mother walked down that road into Tyler, six miles away, almost every morning. There she cleaned houses.

Her husband had died when Earl was in the fourth grade. Her older children worked on the fields of the family farm, planting roses, watering and caring for them, plucking them, then taking them into Tyler to sell. They came back with nickels and dimes and groceries for the younger children.

Earl and one of his brothers slept on a small cot. They walked to a nearby grade school. All the children in the school were black. At that time—the 1960s— most Texas schools were segregated, either all black or all white.

Earl's two older brothers, Willie and Herbert, played football at their all-black high school. Both terrorized ball carriers, bowling them over at the line of scrimmage. Neither went to college because coaches were not interested in black players. In 1969, the University of Texas won the national championship. There wasn't a single black player on the team.

When he was fourteen, Earl didn't care whether he went to college—or to any school. He walked by his school almost every morning and went into a nearby pool hall. A cigarette dangled from his lips as he poked eight balls into side pockets. Thieves and drunks filled the hall. They talked to the burly teenager about making "easy money."

Earl listened. Why should he bend his back under a blazing sun to pick roses? Or sit in a hot schoolroom and sweat over boring books? These men knew how to rob stores and mug people for easy money.

One evening, Earl walked down the winding black-topped road toward the family farm. In his pockets jingled coins he had made while playing pool. Like the dusk coming down, a gloom settled over him. He was trouble, he knew that, missing school so much. Delinquents go to jail, his mother had told him many times. Earl told himself he had become a failure to his mother and to himself. And suddenly, as the old shack came into his view, he remembered a prayer his mother often said: "Lord, lift me up."

He could lift himself up, Earl decided that night, by being as good a football player as Herbert and Willie. New civil rights laws had been passed. Tyler High School, once all-white, now was attended by both blacks and whites. Herbert and Willie couldn't go to Tyler. Earl could. He could try out for a football team that was often among the best in the state of Texas.

At fifteen, Earl stood almost 5'10" and weighed 190. He had stopped playing pool. Each day he ran down the road to Tyler. Each afternoon he crawled on the fields to pick roses. Muscles swelled on his arms and legs. His thick shoulders and broad back were as solid as a wheelbarrow. When he raced against his older brothers, he ran ahead of them, laughing over his shoulder.

He made the Tyler team at two positions. On defense he cruised behind the line as a linebacker. On offense he stormed through lines as a fullback. In Tyler almost everyone was a football fan. Friday night high school games were the big events of the week. And in Tyler cafes and drugstores you heard arguing whether that Campbell boy was better as a linebacker or as a fullback.

The arguments raged even louder in the fall of 1973. Earl knocked down runners and blasted his way into end zones for touchdowns. Tyler won fifteen straight games and the high school championship of the state of Texas.

University of Texas coach Darrell Royal drove from Austin to Tyler. As he drove, he wondered: Dozens of college coaches have talked to Earl. Have they offered him illegal things—like money or a car? Had Earl been bought?

Royal's car stopped at the Campbell shack on the edge of the farm. Inside he saw tattered furniture and cracks in the ceiling. But he also saw things more important. He talked to Ann Campbell and her children. Later he said: "I saw lots of pride in each other—and love. They had an abundance of pride and an abundance of love."

He talked to Earl. He asked, "Have you already been bought?"

The eighteen-year-old Earl looked the coach in the eyes. "Sir," he said, "my people were bought and sold when they didn't have a choice. Nobody is going to buy Earl Campbell."

Earl decided to go to the University of Texas with coach Royal. There, for an English composition course, he wrote: "I want to gain 2,000 yards in one season, win the Heisman Trophy, be on a national championship team . . ." And he told someone, "I want to earn a lot of money so that I can buy my mother a new house. Then, when she lies down at night, she won't see the Big Dipper."

In 1974, Earl's freshman year, he gained 928 yards, more than any Longhorn runner. In 1975, he gained

Earl, as a pro, cuts away from a tackler, then strides into the end zone.

1,118 yards. Texas beat Colorado in the Bluebonnet Bowl and Earl was named the game's most valuable player.

Then came 1976—and woe. He hurt his leg. He had to sit out four games. His weight soared from 220 to 260. He was a gimpy fat man.

Late in that 1976 sason, fat and limping, Earl met a small boy on the Texas campus. He knew the boy. He had seen him at the Baptist church he attended. The boy handed Earl a sign that read, "Keep me going, Lord."

Earl smiled and thanked the boy for the encouraging words. He put the sign on the wall of his room. Each morning the sign reminded him to go out and run, make the leg strong and the fat go away.

By the start of the 1977 season he was once again a lean, 5'10" and 220 pounds. "I feel," he told a pal, "like a 100-pound man in a 220-pound man's suit."

Once again he could scoot like a jackrabbit. "He is as fast as one of those 170-pound scatbacks," Arkansas coach Frank Broyles said. "When you put 220 pounds onto something that fast, you have something no one has ever seen."

In 1976, when Earl was tub of fat, Texas had won only five of eleven games. In 1977, with Earl lean and mean, the Longhorns skewered one opponent after another. Before a big game against Texas A & M, coach Fred Akers whispered to Earl, "I really expect 170 yards out of you today." Earl gained 222 and scored four touchdowns as Texas romped, 57–28.

The unbeaten Longhorns went to the Cotton Bowl on New Year's Day to play Notre Dame for the national championship. Notre Dame jumped out to an early lead. Texas had to pass to catch up. Earl did not get to carry the ball as often as usual—and the Texas passes fell short. Notre Dame won the game and the national championship.

Earl Campbell pops loose from tacklers, keeping low to the ground—one reason why he was so hard to topple.

Earl had not been a member of a national championship team, as he had hoped when he was a freshman. Nor had he gained 2,000 yards in a season. But his total of 1,744 in that 1977 season topped everybody in the nation. He had scored nineteen touchdowns, making him the nation's number one scorer.

And the thing he had hoped to win—the Heisman— he had won. He and his mother flew to New York. There he stood before TV cameras for the first Heisman Show to be telecast. Two former winners, Jay Berwanger and O. J. Simpson, handed the trophy to Earl while his mother stood nearby, smiling at the farmboy who had lifted himself higher than she could have dreamed possible.

Flying back to Texas, Earl told his mother, "Soon I'll be able to build that new house I've been promising you."

The Houston Oilers signed Earl to a contract that paid him a million and a half dollars for four years. Less than a year later Ann Campbell sat in a new house on her farm. It had shiny walls, a fireplace, and four bedrooms.

Behind the house, only a hundred feet away, sat the family shack. Earl and his mother couldn't tear down the old place. Too many memories still floated inside those cracked walls.

Earl remembered the young boy who had hung out in poolrooms. He set aside some of his pro football pay as funds for the Earl Campbell Crusade for Kids. The Crusade helped poor kids in Houston keep out of trouble.

Later in his career Earl played for the New Orleans Saints. But wherever he played, Earl returned after each football season to east Texas and an old shack where he had first found love and pride.

11

Herschel Walker

THE RHINO AND THE POET

Vince Dooley's face was glum. The Georgia coach stood on the sideline and watched another Bulldog drive for a touchdown come to a sudden halt. Tennessee led Georgia, 9–0. Dooley heard the chant from the stands begin once more . . .

"Her-*schellll*! Her-*schellll*!" Georgia fans chanted the name. The eighteen-year-old Herschel Walker, a freshman running back, sat on the Georgia bench. He looked frightened, a Bulldog who wanted to hide.

You have never played a minute of college football in your life. You didn't even want to go to college to play football. You liked to go off and write poems. Why shouldn't you be scared?

The chants—Her-*schellll*! Her-*schellll*!—rolled over the packed Tennessee stadium. Those knots of chanting Georgia fans expected the freshman to save the game. Coach Dooley thought that Herschel one day might be a crackerjack runner. Herschel had been the most highly praised high school runner in Georgia history. He had scored scads of touchdowns. But when Dooley saw him scrimmage against veteran Georgia tacklers, the kid looked stiff. He was as easy to knock down as a board.

Herschel stared up at the huge crowd—95,000 people, more than he had ever seen before, more people than had ever before watched a football game in the south. Fright had paralyzed his legs and arms. If he tried to run, he feared he would stumble and fall.

He heard his name. *"Herschel!"* Vince Dooley's voice. He saw the coach wave him into the game.

He stood. Georgia fans roared. Tennessee fans stared. Now, people thought, we will see if this highly praised running back is a future all-American firecracker or just another dud.

His mornings were much the same when he was a teenager back in Wrightsville. He'd awaken by dawn's light and run up and down the hills above the farms. Then, after the run, he'd sit by himself and write lines of poetry like this:

> *You look for the good days,*
> *While the bad days pass.*
> *The good days pass very fast. . . .*

Herschel was born in Wrightsville in south Georgia on March 3, 1962. He and his six brothers and sisters lived in a spotless white-shingled cottage. The cottage was perched on a small hill that overlooked fields of cotton. Most people in Wrightsville picked cotton, even boys and girls. Picking was brutal, painful work. Herschel's mother, Christine, had picked cotton as a child. She had promised herself no children of hers would have to crawl on their knees in muddy fields. Christine now worked as a supervisor in a factory that made pants. Her husband, Willie, knew the blistering work of picking cotton. He'd sworn his kids would have an education so they wouldn't have to do what he had done. Willie was a worker in a plant that turned Georgia's red clay into chalk.

Christine and Willie together earned better than $20,000 a year. Their kids were well nourished—and not only by food. Their cottage was filled with books. As the children of cotton pickers, Willie and Christine never had the fifty cents or a dollar to buy a book. Willie and Christine wanted their children to have the book learning denied to them.

Herschel was the shortest and fattest child in his fifth-grade class. When he ran, he waddled. When he played, he huffed and puffed as he chased the other boys. When he raced his sister, Veronica, she strode ahead of him, laughing.

During recess, the other kids played games. Herschel sat in a corner and read books.

"He was so quiet," one of his teachers said. "We sometimes wondered if he had some kind of mental or emotional hurt that made him withdraw."

One day, Herschel watched the other boys play football. He asked if he could play. One boy laughed and said, "Herschel, you're too slow, weak, and fat!" The others giggled.

Herschel tapped on the door of the office of Tom Jordan, a gym teacher. Timidly, Herschel asked, "How can I build myself up to play football?"

Jordan suggested push-ups. Herschel did them by the dozen, then by the half-hundreds, and soon by the hundreds. Flabby fat began to harden into lean muscle. He ran with his family each morning. "We all liked to run," his mother said. "Herschel began to run with us for the first time. We'd run along the side of the road. All our children loved athletics. But Herschel, he had to work at it. I don't think it came natural to him."

"We used to compete with each other every day— *every day*," Herschel once recalled. "From the oldest to the youngest, we got mad when we lost."

One day Herschel was doing sit-ups and push-ups. One of his brothers said, "How many did you do?"

"Fifty."

"I can do sixty." And the brother did sixty.

"I can do seventy," Herschel said, glowering.

And he did seventy.

His brother did eighty. Herschel did ninety. The brother did one hundred. "All day we competed like that," Herschel said. At sixteen, Herschel could do one thousand sit-ups and seven hundred and fifty push-ups during an evening workout.

"I'll never forget the day," Christine Walker says. Herschel beat his sister Veronica in a footrace on a dirt road near the house. "Veronica came in the house crying and mad, accusing Herschel of starting too soon. They went out and raced again. Herschel won, and they started arguing again. Veronica was crushed."

She had lost to a good man—at seventeen, Herschel won the state 100-yard dash championship.

By now, a junior in high school, he stood at almost 6' and weighed 210 pounds. He had the thick neck and muscle-slabbed shoulders of a pro wrestler. When he lined up in the backfield for Johnson County High, 160-pound linemen stared with horror on their faces. "I thought he was a lineman, he was so big," an opposing tackle said. "When I saw that mountain rush at me, I wanted to just get out of the way."

He frightened nobody off the field. He spoke so softly that people had to bend forward to hear him. "When Herschel was small," Tom Jordan says, "he was quiet. He didn't change that much when he got bigger. It was almost like he thought his opinion didn't matter. He'd talk to anybody, he'd be so polite. After practice, when all the kids would be cutting up, Herschel would go home to study. He walked home every day with books stacked under his arm."

"When I got to high school," Herschel once said, "I started thinking to myself: If I have a good academic side, people will look up to me. I began to study harder and got to like it."

When riled, though, Herschel could be a terror. During a scrimmage, a teammate grabbed his face mask and threw him down. On the next play, Herschel blasted through the line. He didn't run toward the goal line. He aimed that towering body at the face-mask grabber. He knocked him down. Then he streaked at another defender and bowled him over.

"He looked like an angry rhino," Tom Jordan said. "He went from side to side, knocking over the whole team."

The rhino was leaving a message: don't play dirty with me.

By his senior year, Herschel was the talk of a football-mad state. Georgia high school games draw 15,000 people in towns where the population is only 20,000. Folks had to come early to see Herschel play. In most games, he played only the first and second periods. He scored three or four touchdowns in fifteen or twenty minutes, then sat on the bench for the rest of the game.

"Coach didn't want to run up the scores and embarrass the other teams," Herschel says. "I sat on the bench nearly all the time in the second half. I thought that was a good thing. I felt everybody should have a chance to get into the game."

If he had played complete games, his high school numbers would have gone through the roof. As it was, he scored more touchdowns—86—and gained more yards—6,137—than any running back in high school history. In Herschel's three seasons, Johnson County didn't lose a game.

A Dallas Cowboy scout saw him and said, "He could come right out of high school and play for us."

Herschel didn't want to play football for anybody. An

A student, he thought about going to Officers Candidate School to become a lieutenant in the Marines. He also dreamed about being an agent for the Federal Bureau of Investigation. Two of his cousins worked for the FBI.

"The subject of crime and why people are criminals has always interested me," he once told me. Herschel was also interested in the plays of Shakespeare and the poetry of Longfellow. What definitely did not interest him was playing college football. Life, he told his parents, had to have more important things to it than carrying a football.

His parents wanted him to go to the nearby University of Georgia. Veronica was already there on a track scholarship. His father and mother pleaded with Herschel to join her in college—if not Georgia, then any college. They knew that an education would free Herschel from Wrightsville's fields and factories.

College coaches from California to New York offered Herschel a $40,000 college education if he would play football for them. Herschel listened but promised nothing.

Each morning, running what he called his "joggers," Herschel debated. Should he obey his parents, as he always had? At night he wrote poetry.

"He would say things were fine," his mother said later. "But he'd write a poem about somebody in trouble. I knew Herschel was writing about himself."

In one poem he wrote:

> I wish they could see
> The real person in me.
> Someday I reckon they will know,
> I'm not only here for the show.

He was not here for Saturday shows on gridirons. But he had always been a dutiful son. On Easter

Herschel soars over the Kentucky line on a flight toward another touchdown for the Bulldogs. More often, he tore through a line, tacklers swept aside by a stiff arm as strong as a crowbar.

Sunday morning, 1980, he went out into the hills for a jog. On that run he decided to go to Georgia. He would play football. He would also study criminology. He would graduate with a degree that could get him into the FBI as an agent.

"Her-*schellll!* Her-*schellll!*"

Georgia rooters screamed his name as the frightened freshman ran onto the field. Tennessee's wide-shouldered linemen stared curiously at the freshman they had heard so much about. The Georgia players stared. Could this eighteen-year-old win this game they were losing, 9–0?

Moments later Herschel ran into the line. Two Tennessee linemen smacked him down. Herschel got up, looking dazed. He hadn't dashed as fiercely as he could have into that line. He'd held some of himself back. Fright had dragged him back, he knew it.

On the sideline Coach Dooley stared grimly at Herschel. The coach's anxious face told a story: *Too soon, too soon . . . the kid's not ready yet for big time football.*

Herschel ran out and caught a pass. A tackler slammed him to the turf.

Herschel leaped up. That tackle had knocked the fright out of him, the wanting to hold back was gone. He shot back to the huddle, as loose as he had been when running for TDs back in Wrightsville. This game was the same game he had played in high school—there was nothing to fear.

Late in the game, Tennessee still led, 15–0. Georgia drove to the Tennessee 16. Herschel took the ball. The 6′ 1″, 220-pound Herschel lowered his head and rammed into the middle of the line. A 215-pound tackle hit him—and bounced off to the right. Herschel thundered like a train on tracks over three other linemen. Safety Bill Bates clamped both hands onto Herschel's wide shoulders. Herschel dragged Bates behind him like an old coat into the end zone. A few minutes later, Herschel thundered once more into the end zone. Those two touchdowns were followed by two two-point conversions. Georgia had come back to win, 16–15.

A few games later, Herschel gained 283 yards, the most ever gained in a game by a freshman. In that 1980 season, he rushed for 1,616 yards, smashing the freshman record set by Tony Dorsett. Georgia didn't lose a game. The Bulldogs went to the Sugar Bowl on New Year's Day. They met Notre Dame for the national championship.

Early in the game a Notre Dame tackler smashed into Herschel's shoulder. Herschel fell to the ground, his body writhing, face twisted in pain. The shoulder had been dislocated.

A doctor strapped the shoulder. Pain like a toothache flared down Herschel's arm. He insisted on going back to play. He couldn't raise his left arm. But he could grip a ball with his right. He scored two touchdowns and Georgia won, 17–10. Herschel was voted the game's most valuable player. Georgia was the 1980 national champion.

He finished third in the voting for the 1980 Heisman. The winner was South Carolina's George Rogers, the third straight running back to win since Earl Campbell in 1977. Oklahoma's Billy Vessels had won in 1978, USC's Charles White in 1979. By finishing third in 1980, Herschel had become the first freshman to come so close to winning.

Herschel went back quietly to his studies. He had a B average as a criminology major. "I'm here to get an education and better myself," he once said. "I'm not here to party. Every Saturday on the football field is my party."

The next season, 1981, the Bulldogs lost only once, to Clemson, the eventual national champion. USC running back Marcus Allen gained 2,342 yards that season; Marcus was the first college runner to gain more than 2,000 yards. Herschel racked up 1,891. Marcus won the Heisman. Herschel finished second. No sophmore since Glenn Davis in 1944 had come as close to winning.

The Bulldogs romped unbeaten through the 1982 season. They went to the Sugar Bowl to play Penn State, this game for the national championship. Penn State roared out to a quick lead. Georgia had to begin to toss a lot of passes to catch up—quickly. Since running plays take more time than passing plays, Herschel didn't carry the ball as often as he usually did. Penn State won, 33–3. It was only the third defeat in thirty-six games for Herschel as a Bulldog.

By the end of that 1982 season, Herschel's junior year, he had amassed fifty-two touchdowns, only seven shy of the record shared by Tony Dorsett and Glenn

Herschel stands with the trophy he came close to winning as a freshman (third in the voting) and as a sophomore (second in the voting). Only Glenn Davis came as near to winning three Heismans.

Herschel and Doug Flutie, who learned that Heisman is a synonym for greatness.

Davis. He had totalled 5,259 yards rushing, the most anyone had gained in three seasons. He stood within 1,000 yards, easy striking distance for someone who had averaged 1,700 yards a season, of breaking Tony Dorsett's all-time record of 6,082.

Herschel won the Heisman Trophy for 1982, collecting seven hundred more votes than runner-up John Elway of Stanford. "I thought a lot about the Heisman as a freshman," he later told me. "But I never idolized any of the winners or tried to be like them. I always wanted to be as good as God had given me the talent for being."

As 1983 began, Herschel could look forward to a final season of college football in which he could: 1) Break all the major scoring and rushing records. (He already owned almost a dozen.) 2) Become the first since Archie Griffin to win the Heisman twice.

In the spring of 1983, a new pro team, the New Jersey Generals, offered Herschel five million dollars to turn his back on all those records and honors. Herschel had been dating a tall girl who was one of the runners on the Georgia track team. His sister, Veronica, had introduced them. Herschel and Cindy had decided to marry. They would need money. And for a long time Herschel had promised himself that one day he would buy a new house in Wrightsville for his parents. He wondered: If he were hurt during the 1983 college season, would any team offer him five million dollars?

He decided to take the five million dollars. But he told his professors he was coming back to Georgia during the off-seasons to get his degree in criminology. Then, after pro football, he could be an FBI agent. It was time to make a living, he decided. Or, as he put it in a poem:

It's time to move on,
And give life a try.

Herschel became the best runner in the new United States Football League. In the 1985 season, he gained 2,129 yards, more than any pro runner ever. (NFL runners sniffed that Herschel had played in a minor league—but a record is a record.) He and Cindy lived in a tall apartment building that rose above the Hudson River and faced the Manhattan skyline. One of their neighbors was the Generals' quarterback—Doug Flutie. He and Herschel were close friends. They often joked that there were more Heismans in their apartment building than anywhere else in the world.

I spoke to Herschel one day during the 1985 season. He told me that he still wrote poetry. And he still had his eyes fixed on a career with the FBI or some law-enforcement agency after his football career ended. "But I am really not sure what I will do after football," he told me. "What I hope to be is the very best at whatever I do."

He stared at the cement floor of the Generals' locker room for several moments. Then he looked up and smiled at me. "Being good in anything is easy," he said. "Being great is hard."

Some fifty-odd Heisman winners discovered just how hard.

Index